The State Legislative Institution

The Edward G. Donley Memorial Lectures

Presented by the

College of Law, West Virginia University

First Series, April 29 and 30, 1957

The State Legislative Institution

by

JEFFERSON B. FORDHAM

Philadelphia
UNIVERSITY OF PENNSYLVANIA PRESS

Preface

Man, we like to think, is infinitely perfectible, with perfection always beyond his grasp. The unending challenge is ever before him—the challenge to improve himself and all that lies within the area of his influence. It is in a free society that this is most meaningful to an individual in terms both of personal fulfillment and of social action. It is there that the system affords him greatest scope.

The focus of this work is an area of human organization and activity where, unhappily, the room for improvement is so great that the response of many people is a sense of frustration rather than a strong effort to make things better. I refer to the state legislative institution, the representative arm of a free society. It is not uncommon to hear state legislatures spoken of derisively as if they were hopelessly backward and inept. This is a pretty lamentable situation, to say the least, especially at a time when we depend so heavily upon politically organized society for important decision-making.

We begin with a frank recognition that the state legislative institution is, generally speaking, weak and underdeveloped in power, structure, and procedure. It is, thus, cause for serious concern in our society. To leave it alone, in a sense of frustration, would, however, border on nihilism. The situation is basically one of challenge, extraordinary challenge. This writing represents the limited thinking of one individual as to how the larger community should respond. So great is the need that bold and dramatic action is required. This, in turn, calls for vigorous and articulate leadership as well as basic hard thinking on the subject. Americans today are properly concerned with powerful external forces affecting the future of this country and the human race. It is more important than ever that, at the same time we participate in world affairs, we strengthen our key institutions at state and local as well as national levels.

J. B. F.

Contents

The State Legislative Institution

I

Organization and Powers

of Form and Substance

What is the role of governmental authority in a free society? What, fundamentally, is political power but a means to an end? Within the realm of political concepts, we are accustomed to distinctions between primary powers of government and ancillary powers. In a relative sense, the line is well drawn. The power to provide police protection is primary; the power to tax to finance the police arm is ancillary. In a much deeper sense, I suggest, all governmental power is ancillary; it derives its significance from the individual and group or social values, which it may properly be expected to serve. This stands out clearly in a political community which places its faith in the proposition that governmental authority is derived from the consent of the governed and is exerted for their benefit as individuals and as a group.

Unhappily, it is not solely in totalitarian states that the authority of the state has been looked upon as having independent significance. Once again, in our own national community, we are seeing a fetish made of what, in largely emotive terms, is called states' rights. I refer, of course, to the rationalization of the opposition to full equality of opportunity and equality before the law for our Negro citizens. In the tense situation, which has developed since the public school desegregation decisions, states' rights are invoked as if they were an end in themselves. So vigorously is the doctrine asserted that iteration and reiteration somehow seem to add significance for those who espouse it. It is not difficult to perceive that the underlying concern is with the preservation of a social order. The political argumentation, however, glorifies a conception of governmental authority to the point of serious distortion.

The moral of all this is that it is time to speak calmly but firmly and insistently of the obverse of the coin, which bears the legend "states' responsibilities." Government should be the servant of all the people, not simply of a ruling class or group—racial or otherwise. One makes bold to suggest that the key to the true role of the states and of state power in our system is stress upon states' responsibilities.

If this be so, the natural step is to have a look at state governmental institutions to determine whether they are, in their present state of development, equal to the task. The particular focus of attention in these chapters is the state legislature. What is the record as to the development of this politico-legal institution? What studied efforts have been made to improve it? If the conclusion be that the legislature is undernourished and underdeveloped, the question remains, what should be done about it?

A governmental institution should be viewed in context. In the case of the state legislature, this means both the state and national governmental setting.

Doubtless, the more fundamental considerations relate to the place of the states in the federal system. There are those who are inclined to the view that the states are being relegated to a position of secondary importance in a day of strong centralized government. It is quite apparent that at least three major factors have tended to render more important the influence of the national government in our total scheme of things.

The first of these three factors is the economic development which has made the entire country a great national market and which is characterized by a high degree of interdependence. The second is the international state of affairs with its reflection in a roughly $40 billion defense budget. The third is the fiscal primacy of the national government.

ꭙ The exertion of national power in the economic realm has given the central government a position of extraordinary influence in relation both to production and to distribution. The federal government establishes and administers the major policies affecting agriculture. It regulates the organization and finance of business enterprise, establishes labor standards, and regulates labor-management relations. Many of the major banking institutions operate under its aegis and it asserts significant control of both public and private credit.

These influences are accentuated by policies and activities pursued in the interest of national security in the nuclear age.

(The unmistakable fact of the enlarged role of the central government does not mean that the roles of the state and local governments are proportionately reduced) In many respects, state and local responsibilities have increased. Certainly, that is true as to education, law enforcement and public safety generally, health and welfare, community planning and development, highways and recreation, and, undoubtedly, other functions.

The favored position of the federal government with respect to fiscal powers is regarded by some as the leverage by which states are being pried out of any major position in our governmental scheme of things. The thesis is, in short, that the power of the national purse is such that the government can control activities administered at the state and local levels. I have heard this thinking carried to the point of characterizing participation in state and local government as farm team preparation for the big leagues, so far as any significant role is concerned. This is a serious misconception.

Reflection upon a number of factors should help to dispel it. To occupy a seat in Congress is not to lose one's state and local orientation and loyalties. Despite the prime hold of the federal income tax, more billions in state and local revenues can be and are raised; recourse to federal aid is but one important choice in distributing governmental costs. Man, moreover, is not moved by money alone; there are other influences bearing on policy decisions. There are important and cherished values associated with levels of governmental responsibility close to the people and geared to the reach of particular governmental problems. There are no more challenging problems on the American scene than those engendered by the metropolitan development of our urban life. Clearly, the primary responsibility on this frontier rests upon the states and the local communities.

The simple truth is that the responsibilities of government have increased at all levels. There was a time during the early 1930's when some of us thought that county government was going to be recast in a minor role due to the necessities of resort to state indirect revenues to support traditional county functions. This was a mistaken view. As all of us know, the powers and responsibilities of counties have been greatly increased in recent years to meet the need for urban-type and other services, notably in extramural areas.

Nor has there been any diminution in the responsibilities of the states. They, like individuals, are finding themselves more and more in an interdependent relationship in the total scheme of things. This means not that the states are weak and insignificant but that there is a complex, changing order in the society of governments.

The position of the legislature in the state orientation will be more fully identified in the discussion of powers, structure, organization, and procedures, which will form the main body of the first two chapters. It is appropriate to note at this juncture, however, that the position of the legislature is far from enviable. The executive and judicial branches have the continuity of operation to permit them to do their jobs well. It is a commonplace comment that the legislature is a decidedly part-time institution. In only fourteen states is there a pattern of annual sessions.[1] Generally speaking, biennial regular session are the order of the day, and, in a number of states, constitutional limitations are imposed on the length of sessions.[2] Nor is there any power in the membership in most states to initiate a special session. The occasion for the convening of a special session is typically a matter for the exclusive discretion of the governor.[3] Once assembled in special session, moreover, the legislature in each of twenty-two states may consider only the subjects specified in the governor's call.[4]

The tendency of this treatment of the legislative institution, considered with constitutional limitations on legislative powers and procedure, is to accentuate the role of the executive in the initiation of policy and to reduce the legislature largely to a tax-levying and money-appropriating role.

The American people, during a period spanning more than a century, have been both witnessing and, in a real sense, participating in the deterioration of the position of the state legislature. The present posture of this institution is in marked contrast with its position in the early days of the republic. Perhaps the most conspicuous feature of the first state constitutions was the powerful and pre-eminent position of the state legislature.[5] This, no doubt, marked in part a wide swing of the pendulum away from strong executive authority. Generally speaking, the early state legislatures occupied a dominant position. Well before 1850, however, changes were taking place. There was the influence of Jacksonian democracy with its reliance upon the political role of the common man. There was the understandably popular reaction against the arbitrary and often corrupt exertion of legislative power in aid of private developers, speculators, and otherwise. The panic of 1837 was an influential factor in the modification of state constitutions to limit the power of state legislatures to incur state debt and lend state credit. In the years that followed, there were painful legislative abuses with respect to the affairs of local government and the use of local funds and credits. All this strengthened a popular distrust of the state legislature, which has continued to this day and has left its seriously weakening effect on the legislative institution.

It must be made clear at once that the concern here expressed over the weakness of the state legislative institution is not a form of criticism of the people who have been serving in the state legislatures. Many of them are very able and outstanding citizens and public servants. All are to be regarded on their individual merits. If there is any indictment, it is of the community generally, for organized society has fallen down in the effective development of the basic state policy-making arm.

What renders the present situation the more unhappy is the increased demands society may properly make upon the legislative institution in a relatively mature legal system and in a day of complex human relations and rapid social change. There was a time when the chief instrument of growth in Anglo-American law was decisional law—common law and equity shaped in the long process of adjudication. The situation has undergone great change. Even in the domain of private law, legislation has supplanted the judicial process as the prime agency of law reform. In the enormously expanded realm of public law, with its great body of regulatory measures, policy has been hammered out in legislative halls. This sharply accentuates the increased importance of the legislative process in America.

I suppose that the question which we really face is whether or not we should be content to shrug our shoulders and rock along with a state policy-making branch which has admittedly lost ground both in popular esteem and in power and influence or re-examine the institution with a view to making it a powerful and effective instrument of representative government.

I have no doubt that the correct choice is the second alternative. In recent years, there has been considerable interest in improving the state legislative institution and its processes, and some limited steps have been taken here and there. One notes the emergence of the legislative council as an aid to legislative inquiry and policy formulation. For many years now, legislatures in various states have been assisted by legislative reference bureaus. There are significant drafting agencies and law revision agencies, such as the Law Revision Commission of the state of New York. The Model State Constitution would give constitutional status to a legislative council.[6]

Developments of this character have been well intended and they have made a contribution. I am thoroughly convinced, however, that an agency such as a legislative council is so far from being fundamental in character as to be little more than a palliative. No doubt, some of these things will continue to be useful, but the point that so urgently needs to be made is that drastic action of a basic character is required if our state legislatures are to be equal to the responsibilities of representative government in the days ahead.

A state legislature has a number of functions, but one thoroughly overshadows the rest. The central role of the legislature is policy-making and articulation. This includes the key function of power devolution within the constitutional framework and the business of reviewing administrative performance by executive departments and independent agencies.

If a state legislature is to perform well in this central role, it must have at least four characteristics: (1) broad power proportioned to responsibilities, (2) a relatively simple structure well designed for policy shaping and decision, (3) representation on a basis which is geared primarily to population but is calculated to be responsive to the geographic distribution of people within the state, and (4) continuity of operation with freedom to develop and use effective methodology and procedures.

As can readily be demonstrated, drastic constitutional action would be necessary in this state or that to clothe a state legislature with these characteristics. It is time, however, to have done with palliatives. We should face up to realities and be prepared to make the sustained effort in the way of the public education and political action it will take to vitalize the state legislatures.

I am particularly concerned that the members of the legal profession assert leadership here. The traditional forum of the bar is the courts. It is, thus, readily understood that lawyers are inclined to concentrate their efforts for improvement in legal institutions upon the courts. This preoccupation results in the lawyers leaving it to the political scientists and others to work for improvement in the legislatures. This is not enough. The growing importance of the legislative process and the legislative product in the lives of all of us is too clear to call for elaboration. It is the broad-gauged lawyer, moreover, who should be truly an expert in structure. Thus, of all the groups in our society, I am frankly most concerned with the lawyer in attempting to attract constructive attention to the state legislatures.

Powers. We are all familiar with the theory that under our federal system Congress may exercise only the powers delegated to it by the Constitution, while the states retain all legislative power not so delegated. We all know, too, that, at this stage of our national development and of the judicial interpretation of the Constitution, the reach of the delegated powers of Congress is such that the distinction between delegated and residual powers may appear unrealistic. The theory still holds, however, despite the broad scope of federal legislative power.

Stated a bit differently, state legislative powers are plenary, subject to four classes of limitations:

a) outright or qualified limitations achieved by the delegation of power to Congress by the Constitution of the United States;

b) express limitations in the state constitutions whether to be found in state bills of rights or other provisions;

c) express limitations in the Constitution of the United States on the state legislature;

d) limitations, such as intergovernmental tax immunity, which are implicit in the federal system.

The immediate concern is with part of the ground covered by the second class, namely, limitation found in state constitutions. We are not re-examining federal limitations nor the safeguards to individual liberty found in a state bill of rights. There is a fundamental question here as to the level on which policy determinations are to be made. That question is whether policy decision should be made at the constitutional level or should be left within the scope of action of a representative body. Put a little differently, the question is how far we want to go in relying upon representative government.

Limitation upon the substantive powers of legislatures is of two principal types. The first is constitutional provisions which directly fix policy on this or that matter, which would otherwise fall within the plenary power of the legislature. The second takes the form of prohibitions or restrictions upon legislative action.

I want to consider briefly three examples of the first type. Quite common in state constitutions are provisions dealing more or less specifically with private corporations. The constitution of the Commonwealth of Pennsylvania is illustrative. It contains provisions as to corporate elections, as to the qualification of foreign corporations to do business in the Commonwealth, as to corporate powers in general, and as to corporate powers with respect to finance.[7] It is not evident why the regulation of corporate affairs cannot be left outright to a competent legislative assembly. Regulations of business organization at the constitutional level impair flexibility by precluding policy re-examination and modification in the forum in which deliberate decision-making is ordinarily conducted.

Another example of constitutional provisions which directly fix policy is so-called municipal home rule provisions. This is not the occasion to discuss this interesting subject at any length. Any student of state and local government in this country is, of course, aware of the long struggle of American cities for freedom from legislative tinkering and for broader substantive and fiscal powers. The historic approach has been to try to achieve them by special constitutional provisions. The assumption has been that there was no hope of getting a sympathetic consideration of urban interests by the legislatures in which rural and small community representation was dominant. The advocates of home rule have proceeded on this assumption and have concluded further that life is too short to justify an attack on the problem by reform of the legislature itself.

At the National Conference on Government sponsored by the National Municipal League in Kansas City, Missouri, in the fall of 1954, there was a debate on home rule. As a participant, I, a lawyer, found myself in the rather interesting position of espousing the approach of improving the state legislative institution and its processes in opposition to a panel of political scientists, who favored constitutional home rule and placed their trust in the judicial interpretation of home rule provisions.[8]

What needs to be said here is, first, that local autonomy consists, not in self-determination, but in responsibility for decision and execution within an adequate power framework and, second, that our problem relates to the "how" of assuring the conditions of autonomy without substantial compromise of other values and interests.

The home rule movement has been particularly strong in recent years. Since 1950, six states have added home rule provisions to their constitutions. This has taken place during a period of unparalleled metropolitan growth. Thus, while a commendable effort to assure local units, notably municipalities, that genuine autonomy has been in progress, the actual problems of urban community life have tended to reach across a whole region of which a home rule unit may be but a small part. It is plain that home rule thinking should be related to the problems of metropolitan government. It is not evident how an outright constitutional grant of substantive powers to local units can be made without impairing needed flexibility in attacking the problems of metropolitan areas. Full-fledged home rule as to governmental structure, administrative arrangements, and personnel is another matter.

To achieve the proper balance, we need a climate of opinion—public and governmental—favorable to local autonomy and a greatly strengthened state legislative institution capable of dealing with problems of governmental power devolution on a high level of competence and responsibility.

A third example of what might be called state constitutional pre-emption is dedication by constitutional provision of state revenues. It is understandable that there is strong support for dedication of this or that kind of revenue to particular purposes. This is conspicuously the case with revenues associated with the use of motor vehicles. The movement to have them dedicated to highway purposes has found expression in a number of state constitutions.[9]

No matter how clear the relation between a source of revenue and a particular object of expenditure, dedication by constitutional provision to that object is unequivocally bad constitutionalism. It is obviously a compromise of the political principle of representative government. It is by way of saying that under no conditions is there to be legislative discretion as to the best use of public funds derived from designated sources. Any major dedication leaves the legislature unable to take a whole view in relating revenue resources to fiscal needs.

There is always the possibility of unwise legislative appropriation of funds. If there is to be strong and responsible state government, this risk must be assumed.

For illustrations of restrictive provisions designed to limit legislative power, let us look again to the domain of public finance. Conspicuous here have been constitutional restrictions on the taxing power.

A tax is a device for distributing the cost of government. The greater the freedom of action on the part of the tax-levying authority, the greater the possibility of achieving a tax structure which will distribute the burden in a way which takes into account all relevant considerations. If a legislature is not free to impose a graduated tax on income, for example, its freedom to take into account ability to pay in shaping tax policy is largely restricted. If, by constitutional provision, limits are set on ad valorem levies, a rigid policy conditions what may be done at the legislative level.

In a period of economic depression, it is easy to muster support for property tax limitation. Certainly, that was the case in a number of states in the depression heralded by the stock market crash of October, 1929.[10] In a period of great prosperity marked by high federal income tax rates, one is not surprised to hear proposals for limitation of the federal power to levy graduated income taxes.[11] Limitation of either sort is, again, extremely bad constitutionalism. This is not to embrace any particular tax policy; it is to oppose arbitrary constitutional constriction of the scope of legislative consideration in determining tax policy. We cannot have strong and effective representative government so long as we predetermine major policy choices within the rational range of responsible action.

Another type of fiscal restriction which has been carried to extraordinary lengths in some states is constitutional debt limitation. In Pennsylvania, for example, the limit is, in practical effect, a ban upon state general obligation indebtedness.[12] It takes a constitutional amendment to authorize a state bond issue. Under such a system, the legislature, which simply initiates a consti-

tutional amendment without the power of decision,
may pass the buck to the voters on measures of great
political appeal without tying them to any plan of revenues to cover debt service.[13] This is a curious pattern of
irresponsibility.

What renders a situation like that in Pennsylvania
the more anomalous is that the legislature may create a
public corporation, labeled an "authority," which may
incur large amounts of obligations which are essentially
tax-supported and this without electoral approval. This,
in a word, is accomplished by the issuance of bonds pay-
able from authority revenues in the form of rentals received from the state under a lease of facilities financed
by the authority from the bond proceeds. The rentals
are regarded as an operating expense of the state, and a
continuing contract for operating or current purposes
gets by the debt limit.[14]

Since the authority bonds undoubtedly bear higher
interest rates than would general obligation bonds of
the state, we have a situation in which there is a way to
get around the debt limit, but, mind you, only at higher
cost.

It is to be borne in mind that long-term public bor-
rowing is simply a device for anticipating the revenues
of future years in order to provide a fund for present
use. It is extraordinary that, despite the growing fiscal
demands that state responsibilities make, no serious
consideration has been given to entrusting to the legislatures more power to make use of state credit. At the
very least, the awkward business of constitutional
amendment to authorize particular debt could be supplanted by legislative authorization subject to electoral
approval.

The only conclusion warranted by the realities of the state constitutional order is that the legislatures are hamstrung by numerous limitations on their powers. What we have, in short, is a serious compromise of the philosophy of representative government. There is little prospect of lifting the state legislative institution to the level of quality and performance that we ought to expect of it until we give it man-sized authority. It is responsibility that builds character in individuals and the same can be said of governmental institutions. Responsibility bespeaks commensurate authority.

Yes, it may be granted, as Lord Acton warned, that power tends to corrupt. The safeguards in our system are political checks and balances, the Bill of Rights, judicial review, and the polls.

What we have been doing over a long period is shifting away from the theory that a constitution is an organic instrument which should be confined to fundamentals. The essentials of a written constitution are four things: (1) provisions for setting up the basic framework of government, (2) provisions making the primary distribution of governmental powers, (3) a bill of rights, and (4) provisions establishing procedures for amendment and revision. So far as the legislative branch is concerned, what we have been doing is to freight the state constitutions with a plethora of provisions on all sorts of subjects. In this process, we have obviously shifted the policy-making struggle from the deliberative level of the legislative branch to the level of popular decision by electoral action on constitutional changes. This is a pretty fundamental matter; it involves a choice which has tended to weaken rather than increase the strength of state government. It is time, I suggest, to re-examine this choice. So far as the state legislature is concerned, a return to the theory of constitutionalism, which I have mentioned, would mean that there would be a minimum of constitutional provisions, beyond a bill of rights, operating as limitations upon the policy-making powers and responsibilities of the legislature.

Structure and Representation. We do not have to be told by Alexander Pope or anyone else that the most important element in governmental operations is the quality of the people who hold public position. To say that A is more important than B is not, however, to say that B is unimportant. Nor, I hasten to add, does it mean in the present context that B stands for bicameralism!

Structure is important to the legislative process. It is a matter of erecting a highly appropriate framework for informed, deliberate, and responsible policy determination. It is a matter which, at the state level, urgently calls for our thoughtful, constructive attention.

A characteristic feature of the organization of Congress and every state legislature, save that of Nebraska, is bicameralism. The historical antecedents are, of course, the British Parliament and many American colonial legislatures. Nevertheless, bicameralism is not, historically and traditionally, the only "American way," as some of its defenders vociferously claim.[15] The legislature of Pennsylvania was unicameral from 1777 to 1790.[16] Vermont had the longest experience; it had a unicameral body from 1777 to 1836.[17]

Pennsylvania had a single house during the colonial period, and its retention was advocated by Benjamin Franklin, who said that creating two houses was like hitching horses to each end of a cart and letting them pull in opposite directions.[18] It was abandoned in 1790 because of the strong opposition of the Council of Censors, popular dissatisfaction with the Council of Censors, and the influence of the federal Constitution.[19] The Council of Censors, it is to be noted, was a small elected body with exclusive power to propose amendments to the Constitution and set in motion ratification machinery.[20]

The Georgia constitution of 1777 provided for a single "House of Assembly."[21] Here again, this was in line with the prior experience of the colony and the state. There is some indication that the Pennsylvania constitution was used as a model. Furthermore, it has been said that unicameralism was adopted because of the democratic tempers of the framers of the Georgia constitution. They believed that the people's elected representatives did not need the check of a second house. It was abandoned in 1789 because of the strong influence of the federal Constitution and the desire of the delegates to get the job of constitutional revision over with quickly.[22]

Vermont's constitution of 1777 was copied almost wholly from the Pennsylvania constitution of 1776. Its unicameral body was abandoned in the Constitutional Convention of 1836 by the close vote of 116 to 113. Numerous reasons were given for its demise: popular dissatisfaction caused by the failure of the legislature to choose a governor when no candidate received a majority of the popular vote; constant pressure of the censors in favor of bicameralism; competition for extension of authority with the governor and council; and the influence of financial interests in favor of bicameralism.[23]

Nebraska, of course, is the lone contemporary example of American unicameralism at the state level. There, it was adopted in 1934 and became effective in 1937. The change from bicameralism was made under the powerful leadership of the late Senator George W. Norris.[24] He was aided by the fact that the problems raised by the depression engendered popular dissatisfaction with the existing lawmaking process.[25] Other "live" American examples of unicameralism are the legislatures of Guam[26] and the Virgin Islands.[27]

Nor does the record of American experience with the idea of unicameralism end here. The system was urged in Indiana at the time of the State Constitutional Convention of 1850.[28] Commencing about 1912, proposals for unicameral legislatures have been put forward in more than a dozen states.[29] For example, the system was proposed in Arizona in 1916, only four years after that state was admitted to the Union. The background was a conflict between corporate mining and railroad interests and labor. The proposal was defeated, largely, we are told, because of the voters' preoccupation with other proposed constitutional amendments.[30] In New York, definite proposals were offered at the constitutional conventions of 1915[31] and 1938.[32] In the Missouri Constitutional Convention of 1943–44, a minority report of the Committee on the Legislative Department strongly advocated the creation of a unicameral legislature.[33]

The National Municipal League has been a leading proponent of unicameralism. Its Model State Constitution has put forward the idea since 1921.[34]

Almost all large cities have unicameral legislative bodies, and have had them far many years. The city of Richmond, Virginia, only recently embraced the unicameral form.[35] One notes that the surrounding county of Henrico had, in contesting a Richmond annexation proceeding of 1941, contemptuously characterized the government of the city as an "outmoded, fossilized, bicameral, councilmanic form."[36] It is appropriate to add both that Richmond prevailed in her annexation program and that she took the hint as to the virtues of unicameralism. As for charitable, educational, and business organizations, the thought of a bicameral governing body is nothing short of startling.

Foreign experience should likewise be noted. In Canada, all the provinces, except Quebec, have unicameral legislatures. In Australia, the state of Queensland has a single house legislature. In Switzerland, the cantonal legislatures are traditionally unicameral. Some provinces in Argentina have single-house bodies. Norway, Finland, and Turkey have one-house national parliaments.[37]

State bicameralism is often justified by analogy to the federal system. There were, however, special historical considerations as to the Congress. The Senate of the United States was used as an instrument of federalism; it was not only employed to preserve state identity through representation of the states as such in that body but also used to assure the smaller states effective voice in Congress. There is no parallel here to the situation existing within any state. The great compromise over representation was a major factor in the achievement of a federal union. A state, of course, is a single political entity to begin with; it is not a federation of local units.

The analogy to the British Parliament is equally ill

drawn. The House of Lords has, since 1911, exercised a very secondary role in lawmaking.

It remains to be seen, however, whether the unicameral structure meets the tests for the establishment of a strong state legislative body more effectively than would the continuance of the bicameral structure. What sort of structure is likely to lend itself to the development of a strong, efficient, and able state legislature?

First, and perhaps foremost, there is a need to concentrate legislative and political responsibility. We should avoid a division of authority in the legislative branch of government which permits, and even encourages, buck-passing and deadlock. By concentrating all legislative authority in a single body, we fix ultimate responsibility for the legislative process on its members alone, as well as upon the political party to which the majority of those members belong. The necessary concomitant of responsibility is accountability. If responsibility is diffused, it is difficult to determine accountability. Unicameralism is the structural answer to the problem.

In Nebraska, legislators are nominated and elected on a non-partisan basis. The governor runs and is elected on a party ticket. This certainly concentrates legislative responsibility, but, as noted in a feature article in a recent number of a popular illustrated magazine,[38] the system does not promote executive-legislative teamwork on a party basis not party responsibility for a legislative program.

On behalf of bicameralism, it is said that the second chamber provides a brake against hasty and ill-considered legislation, affords an opportunity for second thought and careful revision, and gives interested persons time to mobilize against undesirable legislation. It is contended that a single chamber would increase the power of a political party machine which controlled it, and that the body would be more susceptible to the influence of any interest group which gained the inside track with the legislative leaders. Finally, it is urged that a single house is more likely to arrogate the powers of the other branches of government and deal oppressively with the people.[39]

All these claims boil down largely to the proposition that the second chamber is desirable because it provides a check. The significance of the asserted check, or balance, is the real focus here. The fact that a second chamber has now and again put the quietus on an ill-considered measure or provision is not alone of compelling import. Had there been but one chamber with the ultimate responsibility, the same result might have been reached there in any instance. One draws little inspiration from the thought that one or the other house may provide a check in the sense of carrying final responsibility in a buck-passing game. Where there is control of one house by one major political party and control of the second by the other major party, the result may be stalemate. So it was in the Pennsylvania General Assembly of 1955 which convened in January 1955, and, due to a deadlock over revenue matters, did not adjourn sine die until May 22, 1956.

There are other things to be said under this head. For example, there is room for the opinion that the United States Senate does not play the traditional role of a brake on the more democratic and volatile lower house and as a protector of property rights. The Senate often appears more receptive to proposals for social legislation than the House. In any event, numerous checks already exist even under the bicameral system. Obvious examples are the executive veto, the courts, and popular opinion. Furthermore, the pinpointing of legislative and political responsibility on the members of a single chamber would in itself act as a check against hasty and intemperate legislation. The members, and the political party to which they belong, would more than likely suffer a severe "check" the next time the voters went to the polls. Finally, the adoption of procedural safeguards by the legislature itself, as was done in Nebraska, can do much to insure that proposed legislation is adequately considered prior to its final enactment.[40]

Secondly, we want to facilitate public understanding and scrutiny of the legislative process. The work of a single chamber is far easier for the public to follow and understand than the business of bicameral legislature, with its dual committee system and its interchamber relationships. Under bicameralism, the conference committee device renders public understanding even more difficult to achieve. This mechanism is the standard means for accommodating disagreements between the two houses, but it, in effect, adds a "tricameral" factor to the already existing bicameralism.[41]

Thirdly, we want to improve the efficiency of the legislative process itself. On behalf of bicameralism, it is said that the form of bills is improved by consideration by two committees and a conference committee on the way to final enactment.[42] That is, at best, a slow and cumbersome procedure, and one that is justified only if it does, in fact, improve the quality of legislation. It is readily granted that in some instances important points may be developed in a second chamber, but the more fundamental consideration is the quality of the regular legislative performance. If a unicameral structure is conducive to more thorough and responsible work on a sustained basis, that far outweighs the chance that a second house will pick up a point of consequence. The awkwardness of bicameralism is stressed by the conference committee device, the *bête noire* of Senator Norris.[43] Traditionally and in current practice, it is the antithesis of legislative deliberation; the committee works in executive session and the two houses take or leave the report of the committee as they find it. If the report is rejected by either house, a new conference committee may be appointed, which, in its turn, may suffer the same fate.

Fourthly, we want a legislative structure which will permit more effective relations with the executive. In the bicameral system, the executive must work with legislative leaders from both houses and there may not be unified party control. In a single-chambered legislature, the executive need work with only one group of legislative leaders, and the lines are more clearly drawn even though his political party does not control the legislature.

Fifthly, we want to fashion a state legislative body of optimum size and to improve the quality of its individual membership. It is almost universally conceded that existing bicameral legislatures are too large. Aside from the obvious matter of increased costs, large size aggravates the problem of getting genuine deliberation. In shifting to a single chamber, a reduction in size would be the obvious expectation and would doubtless be least unpalatable to vested political interests. Fur-

thermore, added prestige and importance would attach to membership in a single house of modest size,
and these factors would be calculated to improve the
calibre of its membership.

Finally, we want a state legislature that is truly representative of all the people. Bicameralism, it is said,
permits the use of different bases of representation in
the two houses, and, therefore, is likely to be more truly
representative.[44] But this is far more fiction than fact.
In reality, most senates and houses are chosen on simi-
lar bases and represent practically identical groups. It
is possible, moreover, to employ more than one basis
of representation in a single chamber. Thus, there
might be single-member districts and some representation at large. Under either system, the fundamental
problem of getting proper voice for people and points
of view is much the same. We shall address this problem of representation in just a moment.

No matter how desirable unicameralism is in theory,
we must recognize that such a proposed change will be
strongly opposed.[45] A poll conducted by the periodical
State Government in 1934[46] showed that, while about
85 per centum of the political scientists and other theo-
rists polled preferred unicameralism, some 85 per
centum of the legislators and other political figures
polled strongly advocated the retention of the bicameral
system. The New Jersey Constitutional Convention
Enabling Act of 1947 expressly precluded consideration of the issue of unicameralism versus bicameralism and urban versus rural representation,[47] even
though unicameralism and greater urban representation had been strongly advocated before the New Jersey Joint Legislative Committee which had been es-

tablished to ascertain the sentiment of the people as to a change in the constitution.[48]

Size and Basis of Representation. The optimum size of a one-chamber legislative body for an American state is not something which can be reduced to precise terms, but we can make an approach to the optimum by thoughtful recognition of certain basic considerations. To begin with, the body should be large enough to have the desired manpower to do the total legislative job thoroughly and deliberately and to be beyond the control of special interests. At the same time, it should be small enough to encourage active participation by the members and to promote free discussion and debate. It must be evident that, if a legislature is very large, resort to parliamentary control will be necessary in order to assure that the business of the body can be prosecuted efficiently. As we are all well aware, the House of Representatives of the United States affords a good example of extremely limited debate in a large legislative body. At the other extreme, a small assembly is much more susceptible to the influences of this or that group. We have learned this lesson in our experience with small state senates.

The Nebraska legislature consists of forty-three members who are known as senators. The constitution left it to the legislature itself to determine the exact number within a maximum of fifty and a minimum of thirty.[49] Certainly, this is a body of modest size and there should be opportunity for effective participation by all members. It is, at the same time, a rather conspicuous target for those concerned with influencing legislative action. One is thus lead to wonder whether the body is quite large enough to absorb external pressures without those forces having a controlling effect. Nebraska is, of course, less populous and less complex in its economic and sociological structure than some of it sister states, but that does not obviate problems of minimum size.

There is considerable diversity as to the size of legislatures, the recognized methods of apportionment and districting, and the methods of reapportionment. The 43-member Nebraska body is the smallest. At the other extreme is New Hampshire, with 424. New Jersey, a populous industrial state, has only 81 legislators in contrast with 280 in Massachusetts. In eleven populous states, which include New Jersey and Massachusetts, as well as California, Illinois, New York, Ohio, and Pennsylvania, the average size is 184.[50]

By far the most common basis of representation in both houses of state legislatures is population.[51] This is generally modified, for one house at least, by a provision of a certain minimum or maximum number of representatives per county or other district. Thus, in Ohio, each county is guaranteed at least one seat in the lower house. In view of the variations in county population, the effect is to compromise seriously the principle of representation according to population.

The next most commonly employed basis of representation is political or governmental unit.[52] In many states, this is the county, but in some of the New England states the unit used is the town. The result in Connecticut, for example, is that the smallest town, even though it has but a few hundred inhabitants, will have one seat in the House of Representatives while New Haven, with a population of 165,000, has but two. This is reminiscent of the rotten borough pattern which once prevailed in England.

Another basis of representation, which is employed in several states, is the privilege of the suffrage.[53] In other words, this basis does not use total population but the number of legal voters in the state. In Arizona, the total house membership is based on the total votes cast for all candidates for governor at the last preceding election.

In no state is proportional representation used with respect to the legislature. As is well known, several large American cities have employed it. New York City abandoned the system several years ago; Cincinnati still uses it. The closest thing to proportional representation at the state level is the cumulative voting plan of Illinois.[54] There, three representatives are elected in each representative district and the individual voter has three votes which he may cast for a single candidate or divide between two or three candidates.

A good deal can be said for proportional representation. It is calculated to assure a fair share of representation to minorities as well as majorities. It operates, moreover, as a more or less automatic scheme of reapportionment among political groups. On the other hand, it does not obviate districting problems; it is not to be supposed that you could avoid cutting the state up into districts of practicable size from a voter's standpoint. The device, moreover, is more suited to a multiple-party system than to a two-party system of politics. In American public affairs, we are strongly committed to the two-party system and it is hardly to be expected that proportional representation would sharpen party responsibility and accountability in state affairs.

Another factor, which is not to be ignored, is that proportional representation is a rather complex system which is not readily understood by the voters.

There has been interest for a long time in the possibility of working out a system of representation on the basis of occupation or function.[55] One recalls that Mussolini organized the short-lived Italian Corporate State on the basis of twenty-two corporations, each of which represented a different branch of industry. The functional plan is grounded on the theory that the various interests of mankind, in the modern state, should be reflected in the makeup of the major policy-making arms of government in terms of economic, social, and occupational status. It is an interesting approach, but how it could be given practical application in a complex, interdependent, and rapidly changing society is more than I can say. The nearest thing to this we have on the American scene is informal representation through lobbyists and other spokesmen who seek to influence legislative decision.

I suggest that the functional plan is both impractical and unsound in principle. To relate representation to particular economic interests is to make it all the more difficult to achieve an overview; it is by way of giving status to a particular economic point of view without formal recognition of groupings in the total community. It is not unlike the commission plan of municipal government (under which the department heads constitute the governing body) in that the legislative policy-makers are associated with particular areas of public interest in the one case and private in the other.

It has been suggested that representation be made on the basis of economic areas.[56] This plan would call for the division of a state into districts which were roughly equal in population and were laid out in such a way as to define the distinctive economic regions of the state.[57] This has some kinship to functional representation. A major difference is the fact that a particular economic area may comprehend a number of important economic activities as well as other groupings. It is to be noted, moreover, that economic development does not fit into nice geographic compartments although certain types of economic activity may predominate in a given area. An application of this, again, would appear to be a very rough and ready plan which could not be applied with anything approaching precision. If the area basis were geared more to urbanization on the one part and rural conditions on the other, the effect might well be a sharper cleavage between representatives from the rural areas and representatives from the cities, and the problem of districting would be continuously complicated by the sprawling suburban and ex-urban development that is going on.

Actual representation is affected both by districting and apportionment. The commonest pattern as to districting is, of course, the familiar single-member district. Where this pattern is used at the national level, we find Congress apportioning the 435 seats in the House of Representatives among the several states but leaving it to the state legislatures to assign the seats by districts. In view of the federal character of the national government, this is likely to involve pretty even distribution of seats by population among the several states. Unhappily, it has operated to create serious discrepancies within a state.

Ultimately, of course, problems of districting, apportionment, and reapportionment will have to be met in the live setting of a particular state. Meanwhile, one may venture to mention a possible approach.[58]

Let it be assumed that we are concerned with a unicameral legislature for a populous state of average area. We posit a membership of from eighty to one hundred. First, we assign a small number of seats for election at large in the state. Then we leave it to the legislature itself to divide the state into regions of substantially equal total population. The remaining seats could be assigned to these regions equally. Within each region, assign one or two seats for election at large. The remainder would be assigned to single-member districts in each region defined by the legislature on the basis of substantially equal total populations.

This plan would mean, as a practical matter, that county and municipal lines would not be respected for purposes of legislative apportionment. It would be true to the principle of representation on the basis of population—the total population to be represented—and it would temper the parochialism of single-member district representation with some state-wide and some region-wide representation. The Model State Constitution would add a requirement that districts be composed of contiguous and compact territory.[59] This is aimed at gerrymandering. That is understandable but it totally ignores factors of geography and population distribution which have no relation to gerrymandering objectives. It may well be better to take the risk of the latter being pursued.

The overriding of county lines in allotting representatives would patently not be easy to accomplish as a political matter. While I would not prefer it, a possible accommodation would be to require that regions and districts embrace a whole county or counties to the extent consistent with the principle of representation on the basis of population.[60]

A satisfactory system of reapportionment is essential to the integrity of a system of apportionment geared to population. We have encountered some difficulty with the policy of leaving it to a legislature to reapportion itself because legislators are human enough to dislike making public decisions directly against their individual interests as such. Legislative inaction on reapportionment is a notorious fact of American government.[61] Several states have demonstrated that the problem can be met by establishing something like a population formula for apportionment and having non-legislative officials apply it in reapportionment after each decennial census.[62] This does not meet the problem of redistricting presented by the plan I have proposed. There appears to be no satisfactory alternative to legislative responsibility for districting and redistricting; marking out divisions of a state for legislative representation is hardly to be left to adminisrative hands. There is reason to believe that a greatly strengthened legislature, as envisioned in what has been said, would give a better than traditional performance in this respect. It might be desirable, moreover, to impose a constitutional duty on the governor to call the legislature into special session for this purpose in the event that the legislature should fail to act during its first regular session after a decennial census.[63]

NOTES

1. 12 The Council of State Governments, Book of the States, 29–30, 38–39 (1958).
2. Id. at 30, 38–39.
3. Id. at 38–39, but note that in twelve states there are provisions by which the legislature may call itself into special session.
4. Id. For a typical constitutional provision allowing the legislature to consider only the subjects specified in the governor's call, see Pa. Const. art. III, § 25. Annenberg v. Roberts, 333 Pa. 203, 2 A.2d 612 (1938), is a leading case illustrative of this point.
5. Green, Constitutional Development in the South Atlantic States, 1776–1860, 88 (1930).
6. National Municipal League, Model State Constitution, art. III, §§ 317–20 (5th ed. 1948).
7. Pa. Const. art. XVI.
8. Bromage and others, A Symposium on Home Rule, 44 Nat'l Munic. Rev. 132 (1955).
9. See, e.g., Mass. Const. amend. LXXVIII; Pa. Const. art. IX, § 18.
10. Public Administration Service, Property Tax Limitation Laws, passim (1934).
11. S. J. Res. 23, H. R. J. Res. 103, 83rd Cong., 1st Sess. (1953).
12. Pa. Const. art. IX, § 4.
13. E.g., Pa. Const. art. IX, § 22.
14. Kelley v. Earle, 325 Pa. 337, 190 Atl. 140 (1937).
15. American Political Science Ass'n, American State Legislatures, 56 (Zeller ed. 1954); Braham, Reform of Pennsylvania's Legislative Procedure, 25 Temp. L.Q. 420, 421 (1952); Carroll, Unicameralism, 11 U. Kan. City L. Rev. 3, 4 (1942); Graves, Is Unicameralism the Answer to Existing Legislative Deficiencies?, 11 U. Kan. City L. Rev. 50, 51, 52, 53 (1942); Two Houses—Or One?, 7 State Gov't 207 (1934).
16. Pa. Const ch. II, § (1776); Watts, Why Pennsylvania Abandoned Unicameralism, 9 State Gov't 54 (1936).
17. Vt. Const. ch. 2, § 2 (1777); Carroll, The Unicameral Legislature of Vermont 2 (1933).
18. See 1943–44 Constitutional Convention of Missouri, File No. 17, 12 (1944).
19. American Political Science Ass'n, op. cit. supra note 15, at 49; Watts, supra note 16, at 54.
20. Pa. Const. ch. II, § 2 (1776).
21. Ga. Const. art. II (1777).
22. American Political Science Ass'n, op. cit. supra note 15, at 49; Saye, A Constitutional History of Georgia, 103, 137, 142 (1948); Ware, A Constitutional History of Georgia, 35, 65 (1947).
23. Carroll, op. cit. supra note 17, at 26, 66–70.

24. See, e.g., Norris, Only One House, 7 State Gov't 209 (1934).
25. Senning, The One House Legislature in Nebraska, 13 Neb. L. Bull. 341 (1934).
26. 64 Stat. 387 (1950), 48 U.S.C. § 1423 (1953).
27. 49 Stat. 1808 (1936), 48 U.S.C. § 1405f (1953).
28. Nolan, Unicameralism and the Indiana Constitutional Convention of 1850, 26 Ind. L. J. 349 (1951).
29. American Political Science Ass'n, op. cit. supra note 15, at 51; Johnson, The Unicameral Legislature, 95–128, 152–55 (1937); Senning, The One House Legislature, 39–43 (1937).
30. Houghton, Arizona's Adventure with Unicameralism—an Anti-Climax, 11 U. Kan. City L. Rev. 38 (1942).
31. 1915 New York State Constitutional Convention, 1 Proposed Amendments, No. 41, No. 232, No. 303 (1915); 1915 New York State Constitutional Convention, 1 Rev. Record 348–51 (1916).
32. 1938 New York State Constitutional Convention, 2 Proposed Amendments, No. 641, No. 306 (1938).
33. 1943–44 Constitutional Convention of Missouri, File No. 17, Minority Report No. 2 (signed by six members) (1944); see also 1943–44 Constitutional Convention of Missouri, Proposal No. 11 (1944).
34. National Muncipal League, Model State Constitution, art. III (5th ed. 1948).
35. 36 Nat'l Munic. Rev. 631 (1947).
36. Henrico County v. City of Richmond, 177 Va. 754, 789, 15 S. E. 2d 309, 320 (1941).
37. For foreign experience in general, see Spencer, Unicameralism: Mile-Post—Not Destination, 11 U. Kan. City L. Rev. 16 (1942).
38. The Legislature Faces the People, Life (April 15, 1957), pp. 40–47.
39. See, e.g., American Political Science Association, op. cit. supra note 15, at 51, 55, 54; Carroll, supra note 15, at 3, 4; Spencer, supra note 37, at 16, 19; 7 New York State Constitutional Convention Committee, Problems Relating to Legislative Organization and Powers, 140 (1938).
40. See, e.g., Dobbins, Legislative Procedure Under the Unicameral System, 11 U. Kan. City L. Rev. 31 (1942); Spencer, Nebraska 15 Years Old, 39 Nat'l Munic. Rev. 83, 84 (1950).
41. Norris, supra note 24, at 209.
42. 7 New York State Constitutional Convention Committee, op. cit. supra note 39, at 139.
43. Norris, supra note 24, at 209.
44. American Political Science Ass'n, op. cit. supra note 15, at 55; 1943–44 Constitutional Convention of Missouri, File No. 17, at 107; New York State Constitutional Convention Committee, op. cit. supra note 39, at 140.
45. See, e.g., Graves, supra note 15, at 50.
46. Two Houses or One? 7 State Gov't 207 (1934).

47. 2 New Jersey Constitutional Convention of 1947, 1473 (1951).
48. Proceedings Before New Jersey Joint Legislative Committee to Ascertain the Sentiment of the People as to a Change in the New Jersey Constitution, 162–68 (1942).
49. Neb. Const. art. III, § 6.
50. The Council of State Governments, op. cit. supra note 1, at 35.
51. American Political Science Ass'n, op. cit. supra note 15, at 31–32.
52. Id. at 34–35, 36–38.
53. Id. at 32–34.
54. Id. at 40; Ill. Const. art. IV, §§ 7 and 8.
55. American Political Science Ass'n, op. cit. supra note 15, at 39–40.
56. Id. at 39.
57. Such a plan has been suggested for the state of California. See Mather, Geographic Basis for a Unicameral Legislature, 248 Annals 236 (1946). The details of Professor Mather's plan are referred to in note 58 infra.
58. A number of proposals for the size and basis of representation for a unicameral body have been advanced. A few are summarized here:
New York—1915 [1915 New York State Constitutional Convention, 1 Proposed Amendments, No. 41, No. 232, No. 303 (1915).]
    1. A "Senate" consisting of 60 members.
    2. An "Assembly" consisting of 168 members, one from each assembly district, and 15 at large to be elected from the counties of New York, Bronx, Kings, Queens, and Richmond.
    3. A "Senate" consisting of one senator from each of the Senate Districts of the state as then constituted.
    —1938 [1938 New York State Constitutional Convention, 2 Proposed Amendments, No. 641, No. 306 (1938).]
    1. A "single house," with members to be elected by proportional representation, and the number of valid votes cast in the several legislative districts. The state to be divided into 13 legislative districts, etc.
    2. "One Assembly" with members from counties as follows:
County of 100,000 population or less—2
County of less than 300,000 population—3
County of less than 500,000 population—5
County of less than 800,000 population—7
County of more than 1,000,000 population—10
Missouri—1943–44 [1943–44 Constitutional Convention of Missouri, File No. 17, Proposal No. 11 (1944).]
    1. A "single House" of such number of members as may be prescribed by law, but not to exceed 81 members. State divided into 34 senatorial districts; each district electing 2 members of different political faith; also one member from each congressional district of the state elected at large.

Boundary of senatorial districts may be altered but no
county shall be divided.

2. A "single chamber" of such number of members as may be
prescribed by law, but not to exceed 75 members. State divided into districts; no county to be divided unless entitled
to more than one member; each district having one to three
members in accordance with population of respective districts.

California—1946 (See note 57 supra). A single house of 96 members. State to be divided into four geographical districts disre-
garding county lines with 24 representatives to each of the four
districts: 1. San Francisco, Oakland, and environs, 2. Metropolitan Los Angeles, 3. Northern and central part of state, 4. Southern California and the southern part of the central valley region.

United States—1958 [Suggestion by Rep. Emanuel Celler of New
York, chairman of the House Committee on the Judiciary, made
on a recent "Youth Wants to Know" television program.]

Merger of the two houses of Congress into one. States would
retain equal representation by the election of two representatives from each state along with representatives based on population. ". . . [T]hereby time, money, duplication of work, and
the pull and counterpull that goes on continually between the
two chambers could be spared. . . . [A] unicameral House would
be more responsive to the people. Nor would the process of deliberation upon which the Senate prides itself . . . be lost.
There would be no duplication of hearings; no duplication of
reports; no duplication of studies; no duplication of debate. . . ."

59. National Municipal League, Model State Constitution, art. III, §
302 (5th ed. 1948).

60. A further concession to political expediency has been suggested.
This would retain the elements which I have suggested above, but
would also add the principle of representation based on county
lines. Thus, counties, or groups of counties, would continue to be
represented as such, along with regional areas (wherein county
lines were disregarded) and the state at large. This suggestion, of
course, would considerably increase the total size of the unicameral legislative body, but need not destroy its balance.

61. Thirty-six states have constitutional provisions designating the
legislature as the reapportioning agency. Two states (Delaware and
Maryland) have no constitutional provision relating to subsequent
reapportionment. Of these thirty-eight states, only fifteen have reapportioned one or both houses since 1950. American Political
Science Ass'n, op. cit. supra note 15, at 44; The Council of State
Governments, op. cit. supra note 1, at 52–56.

62. Arkansas, Missouri, and Ohio. Arizona, while making no provision
for reapportionment of the senate, places responsibility for reapportionment of the house on the County Boards of Supervisors.

In addition, the six states of California, Illinois, Michigan, Oregon, South Dakota, and Texas require reapportionment by an independent agency, but only if the legislature fails to act. Note that all of these ten states have reapportioned since 1950. The Council of State Governments, op. cit. supra note 1, at 52–56.

63. This is the existing requirement in Florida. Fla. Const. art. 7, § 3.

II

The Legislative Process
of Men and Method

In the first chapter, consideration was given to the compelling need of strengthening the state legislature as a key governmental institution. Attention was invited to the weak posture in which we have placed the state legislatures in respect to substantive powers and notice was taken of important deficiencies in legislative structure. The basic thesis developed was that genuine application should be given to the principle of representative government at the state level, that authority should be proportioned to responsibility, broadly conceived. It was stressed that in the implementation of this basic idea there should be structural improvement in the state legislature, notably a shift to the unicameral form.[1]

We come now to a second major division of our subject—the legislative process. Here again, while I am addressing myself to as wide an audience as can be reached through the printing and distribution of these remarks, I must acknowledge that I have a particular concern with the assertion of leadership by lawyers in the improvement of politico-legal institutions and processes. It would be difficult to over-estimate the importance to the larger community of the lawmaking process. Its special significance to lawyers is easily identified. Practically all of the immense and growing body of public law, which includes criminal and regulatory law, is of legislative origin. In the area of private law, moreover, we have seen the legislative process tend more and more to supplant judicial lawmaking. We are, in short, at a stage in the development of positive law and of legal processes in which the legislative process is of first rank importance.

In the past, the law schools have shared the preoccupation of the profession generally with the judicial process. We law teachers would even teach courses in legislation largely by use of judicial cases. In other words, we were looking at the legislative process largely through judicial eyes. That was a sound course, as far as interpretation goes, but there is a great deal more to the subject than interpretation, as many law teachers are now recognizing.

Today, in a number of law schools, the work of the legislatures is being given independent consideration. There is growing concern with the legislature as the principal policy-making organ of state government and the agency, which, within the constitutional framework, distributes governmental power. This is an important development but the community can hardly wait for the present generation of law students to develop into professional and community leaders before doing something about the improvement of the legislative process. I am, thus, led to hope that what is said in this chapter will tend to stir some interest on the part of lawyers and others in this growing public responsibility.

Legislative Sessions. Implicit in the political philoso-

phy of the American Revolution was the proposition
that the representatives of the people should meet often. The Massachusetts constitution of 1780 provides
for annual sessions and expressly declares: "The Legislature ought frequently to assemble for redress of griev-
ances, for correcting, strengthening, and confirming
the laws, and for making new laws, as the common good
may require."[2]

This philosophy did not survive the era of popular
distrust of the state legislature, which, as we have seen,
began over one hundred years ago. By 1900, forty-three
states had abandoned annual sessions.[3] Even today,
only fourteen states provide for them.[4] Generally
speaking biennial sessions are the order of the day. In
a number of states, severe constitutional limitations
are imposed on the length of these sessions.[5] It is scant
wonder that the last twenty years have seen a great increase in special sessions; they have been necessitated
by the normal growth of legislative business, and the
special and pressing problems occasioned by depression, war, and various more localized developments.

In most states, there is no power in the legislatures
themselves to initiate special sessions. The occasion for
the convening of a special session is typically a matter
for the exclusive discretion of the governor. Once assembled in special session, moreover, the legislature in
each of twenty-two states may consider only the subjects specified in the governor's call.[6] This is perhaps
the most direct constitutional affront to the legislative
institution of which we have been guilty. It is to say
that the best interests of the state dictate that the legislature be not entrusted with its general legislative
jurisdiction when in special session.

In a world of ever-growing complexity, legislative policy-making becomes, of necessity, a continuing responsibility. It cannot be properly discharged if it is to be pursued only in alternate years with a long interval marked by inactivity.

This observation is documented (a) by experience with a large volume of bills introduced early in a biennial session which results in loss of legislative time, pending committee consideration, (b) by the congestion and haste in the closing days of a biennial session, (c) by the frequency of special sessions in recent years, and (d) by the development of the legislative council device.

The legislative council is, in effect, a permanent joint committee of the state legislature, assisted by a full-time professional research staff appointed by the council. Its main purpose is to provide the machinery for continuing legislative participation in forming and programming policy in between actual legislative sessions. Today, thirty-six states and Alaska have legislative councils or legislative-council-type agencies in operation.[7] Kansas pioneered in this field; that state established the first legislative council in 1933.[8]

The legislative council movement is very practical recognition of the fact that the state legislature has become a decidedly part-time institution. The device has not failed to make a contribution. We should give it its due. In the larger perspective, it should, nevertheless, be characterized as a patchwork on the governmental fabric. More direct action is needed to strengthen the legislative institution and process.

One step in that direction would be a return to the original American principle of annual sessions without

arbitrary constitutional limitations on their length. On
this basis, a legislature can be relatively continuous, if
need be, and take the time needed for thorough and responsible action at every stage of the legislative process.
On such a work schedule, the legislature would have the
time, at least, to act with independence and maturity
in considering recommendations from the executive
branch, in initiating and developing legislative proposals on its own, and in exercising general oversight
over the execution by administrative officials of policies laid down by statute. Finally, annual sessions
would be responsive to the need for financial planning
on an annual basis.

With a regular pattern of annual sessions, all of the
real advantages of the legislative council device can be
retained while most of its objectionable features can
be overcome.

Arbitrary constitutional limitations on the length
of sessions intensify those evils which are often associated with state legislatures. Bills pile up at the end of
a session and are rushed through without adequate
consideration, debate, and deliberation. A strong minority may take advantage of the short time for deliberation through delaying tactics, and thwart the interest of the majority. In order to accomplish the business
of legislating, the legislature must be enabled to meet
as often and as long as, in the judgment of its leaders,
its responsibilities require. The people's interests are
not protected when the length of a legislative session
is a forbidden topic for legislative determination.

Once we are committed to annual legislative sessions, the question of special sessions diminishes somewhat in importance. Nevertheless, there will be occa-

sions for special sessions, and the legislature itself should have the authority, by action of a majority of the full membership, to initiate a special session. This is not to say that this authority should be removed from the executive; it is eminently desirable that the executive, as well as the legislature, be able to act.

Once a special session has been called, whether by the governor or by the legislature itself, the legislature, like Congress, should be free to exercise the full measure of its constitutional authority in all states of the Union. The legislature is no less competent to determine its agenda at a special session than it is at any regular session.

If we are to have the state legislative institution as a continuing body, we must face up to the fact that salaries of individual legislators should be commensurate with the time and personal sacrifice involved in their service. It is true that there is not necessarily any correlation between high salaries and superior laws. Nevertheless, legislative salaries are inadequate in most cases.[9] Robert Luce some years ago ventured the following criterion for the payment of legislators: "The pay of a state legislator ought not to be large enough to make it a material factor in candidacies for the position.

"It ought not to be so small as to impose real hardship on a man without resources."[10] This puts the need of adequate pay very cautiously.

Here again, our familiar *bête noire,* the constitutional limitation, comes out to plague us. In approximately half the states, legislative salaries are fixed by constitutional provision.[11] The assumption, of course, is that legislators are human, and all too subject to temptation if given the power to increase their own compensation. It should be enough to make any increase ineffective until the next term of office.[12]

No matter how fixed, any realistic salary scale must take into account the factors of increased time devoted to the business of legislating and decreased time devoted to private business or profession. Perhaps it is impossible to compensate the member in full for his time and sacrifice; nevertheless, a more realistic approach must be taken toward the problem if we are to have basis to hope that we can attract more men and women of ability and experience to the state legislative chambers.

It may not be amiss here to refer back, for a moment, to the matter of the unicameral structure. There it was pointed out that added prestige and importance would attach to membership in a single house of modest size. Members of Nebraska's unicameral legislature bear the title "Senator." Things of this sort may compensate to some extent for financial sacrifice.

We come now to a consideration of steps which may be taken to strengthen the legislative process within the annual session framework. Central to this part of our inquiry is, first, a consideration of constitutional specification of legislative procedure and, then, an examination of the standing committee system.

Constitutional Specification of Legislative Procedure. One might suppose that a deliberative body entrusted with great powers of state might be competent to fashion its own rules of proceeding. That is the approach of the Constitution of the United States with respect to the Congress. The federal Constitution does speak to organizational matters, like legislative officers and quorum, and requires the keeping of journals.[13] It specifically requires a yea and nay vote entered on the journal only in one situation—the reconsideration of a bill after veto.[14] The governing policy of the Constitution is to empower each house to determine the rules of its proceedings.

In the state constitutions, the tendency has been to cover not a little of the procedural ground by constitutional specification. Some of the requirements are outmoded; others may have some rational and policy basis. Here again, the tendency has been restrictive.

The familiar state requirement of reading of a bill at length in each house on three different days is so clearly outmoded and unwise that it deserves but scant notice here. It is safe to say that legislators of this day can read, but I would not hazard the opinion that they could stay awake during a clerical droning of all the provisions of a long bill. These days, printed copies of bills are promptly available to members for information and study. Time for deliberation can be afforded by rules governing the staging of consideration of bills. State legislatures have no choice as to existing reading requirements; they have to violate them in order to get their business done.[15] In this context, one is startled to find reading requirements in the latest edition of the Model State Constitution.[16]

Provisions requiring the printing of bills and that copies be on the desks of members in final form for a minimum period prior to final passage are not uncommon.[17] The same is true of requirements that bills be referred to committees.[18] These steps are obviously desirable but why clutter a constitution with them? House rules can readily cover the ground.

Overspecification of provisions, with respect to compelling attendance and testimony of witnesses and the production of papers, instead of constituting a helpful grant of authority, may, in effect, be restrictive because narrower than the power to be implied in the absence of express provisions.[19]

State constitutions abound in provisions forbidding amendment of a bill which will alter the original purpose,[20] requiring unity of subject matter in a bill and exacting that the subject of a bill be clearly expressed in its title.[21] The first and third are technicalities of scant policy content; yet, in a state in which the courts consider them mandatory and judicially enforceable, they provide arguments for the lawyers and hazards for statutes otherwise duly enacted. The ban on amendments changing the purpose is designed to assure full deliberation on the stuff of a measure. The object is good but I prefer my faith in a body of able representatives than in hard-to-apply procedural restrictions. The title requirement has little point; its practical significance in giving notice to legislators and others is very limited. There is no parallel provision in the federal Constitution; yet people manage to find out what congressional bills are about.

The unity of subject provision has genuine policy content.[22] It bespeaks separate consideration of unrelated matters and, thus, is designed to bar log-rolling. That is in keeping with a philosophy of focusing legislative and executive responsibility. That it generates problems in practical application, which are good grist for litigation, is equally clear.

What has been said about constitutional requirements and restrictions with respect to legislative procedure confirms the proposition that we have burdened state constitutions with details. This, I repeat, is poor constitutionalism. So far as the legislative institution is concerned, the effect has been enervation of power, and impairment of freedom and efficiency in procedure.

The Standing Committee System. To require, as some state constitutions do, that bills be referred to committees before consideration by the body is surely a work of supererogation. Resort to committees is inescapable, in any event. A deliberate body of any size is simply not constituted to do the work required in the way of inquiry, hearing, drafting and redrafting, and intensive analysis to prepare and mature a legislative proposal for debate and vote. This is enough to suggest that the strength and effectiveness of the system of standing committees is vital to a quality performance of legislative functions. This conclusion would hold even if the work of a committee were largely the sifting of bills referred to it. If, as I suggest, a committee is to have a hand in the initiation of policy and to bear responsibility for review of administrative performance in the execution of legislative policy, its key role becomes doubly clear.

Since a legislature is, in a word, an arena for a policy struggle, the capacity of those with the responsibility and authority for decision to evaluate the influences at play and to achieve a real measure of independent judgment may be a critical factor. This capacity depends heavily upon the strength of committees and the thoroughness of the work. Weak, ill-informed committees are no match for a highly organized lobby with a wealth of data and arguments.[23]

Let us now briefly examine the standing committee

system as it is presently constituted in most state legislatures.[24]

We note at once a great proliferation of committees. Large membership is not uncommon. The results of this are duplication, confusion, waste of legislative talents, and the absence of clear-cut responsibility of each committee for legislation in an assigned field. Committees have been created in the past to consider areas of legislation which have declined in importance; subsequently, new committees have been created with overlapping jurisdiction; but the existing committees linger on largely because of the desire of members of the legislature for committee chairmanships and the assumed prestige of membership on numerous committees. The individual legislator finds himself serving on more committees than limitations of time and capacity permit. Conflicts in the times of different committee meetings often prevent attendance by members, sometimes to the extent that a quorum cannot be mustered. Furthermore, the great bulk of work in most states is done by only a few of the many existing committees. These committees are often assigned more work than they can adequately handle whereas minor committees languish with little to do. In keeping with the congressional practice, important posts of committee chairmen are often awarded on the basis of a hard and fast rule of seniority.

In most states, standing committees go out of business when the legislature adjourns sine die and have no legal status until the legislature reconvenes.[25] They exercise no investigatory powers, even within the areas of their jurisdiction. They are given no authority to review the administrative performance of executive departments and independent agencies, even with respect to powers and duties of these agencies which emanate exclusively from the legislature. It is true that the legislature will, from time to time, conduct investigations. But these are usually entrusted to select committees appointed solely for the purpose of conducting the particular investigations. Existing standing committees exercise no such jurisdiction, even though matters under investigation fall squarely within the areas of their jurisdiction.

As a gauge of state legislative committee conduct of hearings, a passage from George Galloway's *The Legislative Process in Congress,* serves us well:

Committee hearings are considered to be well organized and conducted when they meet the following standards: adequate advance notice of the hearing has been given to all interested parties; advance copies of their statements have been obtained from prospective witnesses and briefly digested for the information of committee members; witnesses have been informed what the committee would like them to cover in their testimony; the assembly and disclosure of all pertinent information have been encouraged; the order of appearance of witnesses has been so planned in advance as to promote a logical development of the case; committeemen have been briefed on the objectives of the hearing, the testimony to be heard, and the pertinent questions to be asked so as to elicit all relevant information; committee members who are not adequately prepared refrain from asking irrelevant questions, allowing counsel to develop the case; and joint hearings are held by the parallel committees of the two houses on common problems so as to avoid duplicating testimony and save the time of all concerned. [26]

Committee practice, of course, varies, and it is impossible to generalize with complete accuracy. Perhaps a reasonably reliable statement of what usually takes place can be achieved. When a bill has been introduced, it is normally referred according to its objective to the committee which by virtue of tradition has been given cognizance of bills dealing with that subject. The committee chairman then becomes responsible for seeing that it is brought up for consideration and, in his discretion, for determining when a committee meeting will be held at which the proposed bill will be considered. Normally the committee will have no fixed meeting schedule. It is common for committee chairmen to refer bills to subcommittees for study as soon as they are brought up for action at committee meetings. More often than not, the committee, or subcommittee, as the case may be, will have no professional research staff under committee control to aid it in its study of the proposed bill.

Committee members, even if capable and experienced in the field under consideration, have limited time and no staff at their disposal for investigation of proposals before them. Thus, of necessity, committee members can inform themselves as to the merits of a proposed bill only through the medium of public hearings at which interested groups appear and are heard. In many states, the rules require no notice of public hearings, and the question of notice, and for that matter whether a public hearing will be held at all, is largely left to the discretion of the committee chairman. As a matter of actual practice, public hearings are usually held on bills in which there is general public interest or which produce specific requests for hearings. Some states, however, require public hearings on all bills; but here, hearings on bills in which there is little public interest are marked by sparse attendance, or by the absence of witnesses altogether and, thus, become nothing but a mere time-consuming formality. Often, public hearings are not well organized. Those seeking to be heard may be asked to give their names to the committee clerk and indicate whether they wish to speak for or against the proposed bill. After the conclusion of all testimony, the committee will take the bill under advisement and reach a final decision in executive session.

Let us assume that there have been well-organized hearings at which intensive data and opinions are presented. What use is made of this material; what records are kept and reproduction made? The congressional pattern is a matter of common knowledge. A full record is made of hearings conducted by a subcommittee. The complete record is made available for study by the subcommittee and by the parent committee. The Legislative Reorganization Act of 1946 makes hearings and other committee records the property of Congress, available to all members. Each standing committee is authorized to have testimony and other data, submitted at hearings, printed. This is done as to any matter of substantial interest and the material thereby placed at the disposal of the public as well as the membership.[27]

In Congress, oral reports of committees are not in order. Nor is a report a mere formal statement of committee action. What we have is a supporting textual statement, which digests the provisions of the bill in non-technical language and sets out the reasons for the committee recommendation. Minority reports which present reasoned opposing statements of position on bills are not uncommon.

This contemporaneous legislative history is of great significance both for Congress in the internal legislative process itself and for the general community in the administration of statutes after enactment. Within Congress, it roughly resembles the record on the basis of which judicial and administrative adjudications are made. Along with the recorded floor proceedings and debates, the committee records, hearings, and reports constitute the formal record basis for legislative decision-making. In the application of statutes, legislative history is a much-used extrinsic aid to interpretation. This is so much the case that efforts are made to shape legislative history with the object of laying the groundwork for a desired interpretation directly in mind. Such a course is more subtle than fighting for plain language in the text of a measure. It is even pursued with joint resolutions to initiate constitutional amendments. The majority report on the 1956 Dirksen version of the so-called Bricker Resolution relative to the treaty power is a lively example of this.[28]

The state situation as to the important components of legislative history is a very different story.

State courts do resort to legislative history in statutory interpretation. The familiar formulation is that recourse to such extrinsic aids may be had where statutory language is ambiguous.[29] There is, however, a paucity of cases in which the state courts have actually turned to legislative hearings and committee reports for guidance. The explanation is that in most states no official verbatim record is kept of the testimony at committee hearings; and the final committee report, even when recorded, often amounts to nothing more than a mere recommendation, without inclusion of the committee's reasons for its action.[30] I have seen committee reports which were nothing more than identification of the bills and of the committee action on a little two or three-line printed form. A bill would be reported "favorably," "unfavorably," or (in some states) "without recommendation." There are, of course, instances of specific inquiries made by special committees in which full-panoplied legislative histories will be recorded and published. This is done on an ad hoc basis.

Committee reports are printed in full in but a few states.[31] But it is not just in the lack of recording that the difficulty lies. It probably rests on the fact that the committee stage is for most legislation the most important, yet it is the stage regarding which the least information may be obtained from existing legislative records. Many abbreviated committee reports to legislative bodies are explained and supplanted upon the floor of the legislature by oral statements by the committee chairmen, but these are not recorded in the legislative journals. Only in Maine and Pennsylvania are proceedings in the two houses fully recorded and published. Several legislatures distinguish between reports of standing and special committees, printing the latter in full but only the recommendations of the former. Many legislatures print the reports of conference committees in full, although these usually contain only the text of proposals for accommodation of differences between the two houses on pending bills and thus tend to be of even less value than the reports of standing committees.

Let us be more specific and note the practice in two or three states.

In Iowa, "there is no permanent and complete record of committee proceedings, but in most committees some notes are taken in a haphazard fashion. The committee chairman is the custodian of these notes until the bill is reported out; they are then turned over to the clerk of the proper house, and are ultimately boxed and placed in the history department of the state archives. No attempt is made to keep these records in any semblance of order. Aside from these meager records, what occurs behind the committee doors when the members are considering a proposed bill is left to the conjecture of the other legislators and the courts. . . . Nowhere in any published journal or report can the reasons for committee actions be found."[32]

In Missouri, the records kept of legislative action are very perfunctory. The house and senate journals merely "record the reading of bills, disposition to committees, simple committee recommendations, and whether or not the bill passed. No transcripts of the debates, which would indicate what the legislators were actually thinking, are kept."[33]

Again, "Kentucky does not publish committee reports, nor the debates and remarks of the members of the legislature on the floor or in committee hearings."[34]

In New York, where conscious efforts have been made in recent years to improve the legislative process, the debates are recorded but are not published.[35] Recently, Mr. W. Maldwin Fertig, who has served as counsel for governors Franklin D. Roosevelt and Herbert H. Lehman, made a vigorous plea in a letter to the *New York Times* for a state publication, which, like the *Congress-*

ional Record, would reproduce legislative debates in full. His description of the present situation is very engaging.

If one wishes to obtain a transcript of the remarks made during a debate on any particular measure he can obtain it at fixed stenographic rate provided—believe it or not— that consent is first obtained from the member of the Assembly whose remarks are to be transcribed.

As to the Senate, a full typewritten copy of the debates is on file but can be read only by travel to Albany, or having someone copy the desired portion of it by longhand or shorthand transcription. I understand that portions of the debate may be obtained on the basis of a fixed stenographic charge, but unlike the Assembly, the censorial power of a Senate does not obtain.[36]

His letter was followed by one from Ernest H. Breuer, the state law librarian, which tells us that the situation is worse than Mr. Fertig supposed. Mr. Breuer had this to say:

I am reliably informed by the Senate itself that by resolution passed at each session the official stenographer of the Senate is directed to transcribe the daily debates of the Senate and a copy is filed and made available only to members of the press, including radio and television, for inspection. It is not open to public inspection. Furthermore, the censorial power of each member of both the Senate and Assembly prevents anyone from getting a transcript of a member's remarks without the specific comment of the member concerned.[37]

We have seen that as presently constituted and operated the standing committee system is a pretty meager development. More often than not, no official record is kept of testimony at public hearings before committees. On the basis of this testimony, the committee in executive session will often make significant changes in the proposed legislation; yet the committee's reasons for such significant changes are not a matter or record. The committee's final report may be nothing more than a "yes" or "no" recommendation; and even if the committee's recommendation is subsequently amplified on the floor, the statement will not be recorded in the legislative journal.

The first step in fortifying the committee system is the erection of a rational committee structure. The various areas of legislative jurisdiction should be marked out with reasonable clarity and assigned to standing committees on a fairly even basis as to amount and importance of work. It is believed that a sharp reduction in the number of standing committees could be achieved with a corresponding reduction in the assignments of individual members. It is true that the experience of Congress might be repeated. What has happened there is a great increase in the burden of subcommittee work within the so-called streamlined committee system. Even so, there would be a greater concentration of an individual member's effort and greater likelihood that he would achieve real grasp of the problems and approaches in a given area of legislative concern. The simple primary committee pattern would be conducive to the orderly and systematic conduct of committee business unhampered by conflicting demands upon the time of the members.

The ability and responsibility of committee members, and particularly committee chairmen, should play a greater part in their selection. Tenure and experience are, of course, important. Seniority, however, is no substitute for character and competence. The seniority rule has been known to place people of meager qualities of mind and character in key roles. I am unhappy with it because it is not more sensitive to merit. At the same time, the problem of developing a better method presents great difficulty. With some diffidence, I suggest that committee chairmen be elected by the membership from a list of experienced members. Eligibility for election could be confined to members who had served on the particular committee for a stated minimum period calculated to afford the needed experience.

It is a major function of the legislative rules to guide the conduct of committee work. A committee is a child of the parent body; it should have parental direction as to the essentials of efficient, fair, and thorough performance of committee functions. Obviously, the parent has been a bit lax. Even when excellent public hearing practices have been developed, they very often are not incorporated into the rules.

Rules should provide for advance notice of committee hearings and for the making of a complete and detailed record of all committee proceedings, including the final recommendation of the committee, together with the reasons therefor, and how the individual members voted. As we have seen, the failure of the state courts generally to resort more frequently to committee reports and legislative journals in interpreting statutes is due primarily to the inadequacy of the records of legislative proceedings kept by the states. Procedurally, these records should be produced in both greater quantity and greater detail; substantively, they should contain more than mere recommendations. Whether committee reports will be used widely in the future by state courts will depend in small measure upon the way in which they are prepared and the technical skill which is at the service of committees in the drafting, first, of the statute under consideration and, then, of the report which explains it.[38]

Improvement in the preparation, recording, and content of state committee reports is desirable not alone as a means of assisting the courts in interpreting statutes. Preservation of accurate records might encourage or avoid subsequent repeal of statutes, especially where it can be shown authoritatively that the reasons which obtained for the original enactment are still or no longer present.[39] Finally, it would assist subsequent legislatures in matters considered, but not acted on, at earlier sessions. A complete record makes the reasons for action on the part of the legislature matters of public record, discloses what the legislature and its standing committees are actually doing, and, thus, tends to fix legislative and political responsibility. It is relatively easy to reach a conclusion when the reasons leading to that conclusion need not be reduced to writing and become a matter of record.

Consider the analogy of the work of appellate courts. If a conclusion is sound, it can be supported by a reasoned statement that holds together. A judge who is assigned to write the opinion in a case may find that the result already agreed upon by the court in conference does not stand the test of the close reasoning he gives the matter in working on a draft of opinion. So, intellectual honesty impels him to take the case back to his brethren for further consideration.

A legislative committee is concerned with policy decision in a political atmosphere, but the judicial analogy, even so, has some bearing. Men and women of integrity are not chaff to be blown about by every puff of the political winds. In a framework calling for reasoned exposition of the basis of policy judgment, they may be expected to measure their thoughts and their words.

The procedural rules should also require prompt consideration of all measures referred to committees, provide for the establishment of an effective and workable discharge rule by means of which the legislative body may prevent the arbitrary pigeonholing of a bill by a committee which is determined not to report it. The latter matter has engendered much controversy. A common practice seems to be to provide that a committee can be discharged from consideration of a bill only by a majority vote of all members elected;[40] and often this can be initiated only by the author of the bill after the committee to which the bill was referred has failed to act within a stipulated time. In contrast, the Missouri constitution of 1945 provides that a bill may be recalled from committee by a vote of one-third of the members elected.[41] There is a danger of political manipulation in the Missouri system in that the minority political party might be in position to force every bill to the floor. It may be doubted, however, that this is of great moment.

It seems appropriate to consider at this juncture the role of permanent legislative service agencies.[42] Reference to them was made in the first chapter. There, the position was taken that a legislative council is a palliative to which a number of states have resorted in recognition of the weakness of the state legislative institution.

I reaffirm that thesis here. It must be made clear at once that this is not an attack on service agencies, as such. The total staff job of a legislative service group should be comprehended, structured, and manned. There are choices of organization and method. I hold no brief against separate agencies such as reference bureaus, code revision and law revision commissions, bill-drafting services, and legislative budget offices. They are consistent with a direct effort to strengthen the legislature proper. Most of them can be very useful even in the populous states where the volume of legislative activity justifies substantial staff resources for all the standing committees.

A legislative council, which is assigned responsibility to shape and put forward legislative proposals, is a different kind of agency. It may be granted that it has made significant contributions. It has provided a research staff on a continuing basis. It has approached problems from the point of view of the legislative branch of government. Its members are members of the legislature itself; the members of its research staff are employees of the legislature, not of the attorney general or some other department of the executive branch of government. It has, moreover, performed a valuable educational function by informing the general public on imminent problems and issues. This is done through the media of holding open public hearings, and the wide distribution of studies and reports prepared by the research staff.[43]

Nevertheless, the legislative council device is an improvisation born of an awareness of the lack of continuity in the work of state legislatures and the weakness of their standing committees. The sound course is to put this device aside, while retaining its desirable features, and concentrate on strengthening the basic institution so that through its regular committee and other procedures it can perform with high competence its tasks of policy formulation and oversight of administrative performance. Pertinent here are the continuity and investigatory authority of standing committees.

With respect to continuity, it should be made clear in the constitutional framework of a particular state that a legislative house is competent to have standing committees continue their work in the interim between sessions. The general but not universal judicial view at present is that a legislative body becomes *functus officio* upon sine die adjournment, as a consequence of which no part of the body, such as a committee, is competent to go on with its business. We should have done with this legalistic restriction upon legislative continuity of action. Consideration should be given, moreover, to the bearing of interim responsibilities upon the problem of legislative compensation.

The power to investigate, with authority to compel attendance, produce documents, and testify, is an important adjunct of the legislative power. If a standing committee is to be equipped to perform the assignment of fact-finding, sifting, policy-shaping, and oversight of administrative area, it should have this power. The haphazard business of using select committees for investigations, and mustering them simply as public emergency or political expediency provides an occasion, is spectacular. What it contributes to the steady responsible conduct of legislative business is, however, a question. What is needed is a standing committee system which performs thoroughly the steady job of policy determination and review of administrative performance.

I am very sensitive to the risks of abuse which attend the exercise of legislative investigatory authority. The dangers of unfairness and serious hurt to individuals are very real; members of the executive branch and independent administrative agencies can be needlessly harassed. This point is accentuated by the fact that applicable constitutional safeguards for the individual do not fully cover the ground. There is, for example, no clear judicial assurance that one called before a legislative committee to testify as to matters affecting his reputation and economic well-being, or even his liberty, has a constitutional right to counsel. This gives one pause. The answer, nevertheless, should not be a compromise of legislative authority. What is indicated is legislative restraint expressed in rules of fair procedure laid down to govern all committees. After a deal of experience in Congress with investigations, much of which does the legislative branch no credit, we have made progress in bringing about a responsible attitude of legislative restraint. This has been achieved in the operations of particular committees; there are still no adequate general rules of fair procedure in either house.[44]

A committee system reorganized and strengthened in these respects will improve the legislative process generally and, in addition, will constitute a vehicle through which those specific aims which we have previously mentioned can be achieved. Thus, it will be capable of initiating legislative policy on its own, thereby making available to the legislature, as a whole, policy which has been conceived and initiated by the legislative branch, not by the executive branch or the majority political party leadership. It will be capable of sifting recommendations for legislative action received from the executive, and giving the legislature a well-considered judgment on their merits. It will be in position to make periodic review of the performance by administrative agencies of important functions delegated to them by the legislature. Finally, it will materially assist in keeping lobbying in proper balance.

Meanwhile, we shall be experiencing the same sense of frustration about legislative business that has so long disturbed earnest students of government. The legislatures, by and large, will, due to their weakness in power, organization, and the policy-making process, continue to be the too-easy prey of outside pressures and party politics. We shall continue to witness legislation by party caucus instead of genuine deliberation and informed decision-making.

It is interesting to note that many of the things that I have discussed have been accomplished within the framework of Nebraska's unicameral structure.[45] In Nebraska, there are only eleven subject-matter or bill-considering committees. This means that in a forty-three-man legislature, with nine-man committees, each member need serve on only 2.2 standing committees. In general, bills appear to be distributed fairly evenly among the eleven standing committees. Seniority plays a part in the selection of committee chairmen. But an experienced member always heads each committee, and the more important committees usually have few freshmen members. When a bill has been introduced and referred to the appropriate committee, the committee chairman no longer has discretion to call it up when he chooses without notice; the committee on committees is required to arrange and publish a schedule of regular standing committee meetings in such manner as to avoid, as far as possible, conflicts in the assignments of members to such committees. In practice, meetings are so scheduled that each member serves on a committee every afternoon during five days of the week while the legislature is in session. Notice of date and time of committee meetings is published in the legislative journal five days in advance and placarded on blackboards in the lobby; the number of the bill or bills to be considered at the meeting is given. Committees must hold public hearings with five days of advance notice. Executive sessions, after public hearings, are open to the press. When bills are reported out of committee, the committee must submit a brief statement of the main purpose and intent of the bill, the reasons for the committee's action, and minority views, if any. This statement is posted in members' files, along with the printed bill as originally introduced, for reference when the measure comes up on the floor for final action.

The picture in Nebraska is far from perfect. For example, the standing committees have no authority to function when the legislature is not in session; they have no investigatory power; while required to submit a "brief statement" when reporting a bill out, there is no record kept of the testimony at public hearings, and indications are that the "brief statement" is just that. Nevertheless, real improvement is apparent.

Popular Legislation—The Initiative and Referendum. This is not the occasion for a full-dress independent examination of the initiative and referendum; our immediate concern is simply with their relation to the strength and effectiveness of the legislative institution.

It will serve to refresh recollection as to the nature

and operation of these devices to borrow a passage from an earlier discussion of the subject:

The initiative is a device by which any person or group of persons may draft a statute and, by securing to a petition the signatures of a minimum number of qualified voters, require the appropriate state officials (with or without action upon it by the legislature) to submit the measure to the electorate at a general or special election. If an initiated measure is approved by the required majority, it becomes a law. In some states the device may be employed to amend the constitution. The true initiative has two forms. The direct initiative gets a measure to the voters without the necessity for first submitting it to the legislature in order to permit consideration there before referral to the voters may be required.

The referendum is a device whereby a measure, already adopted by a representative legislative body or constitutional convention, is held in suspense until it shall have been submitted to the voters at a general or special election, there to be ratified or rejected by majority vote. There are compulsory, voluntary and optional types of referenda. In the case of the compulsory referendum a measure must go to the electors and receive a majority vote before it may become operative. This type is used to a great extent in the amending of state constitutions. The voluntary type is referral to the voters by the legislature at its own instance. Under the optional form a referendum is held responsive to a petition of a percentage of the electors. It is the optional type which is usually embraced in the combination of the initiative and referendum.[46]

These methods of popular participation in lawmaking were conceived as means of assuring consideration of proposals when the legislature would not act and of vetoing legislative action out of keeping with prevailing opinion as gauged by the voting at a referendum. They had their greatest appeal early in the century, notably during the so-called progressive ear from 1910 to 1915. Over one-third of the states have embraced them but none since World War I.[47]

It is clear to me that we have here another manifestation of the spirit of distrust of the state representative lawmaking body. The net effect is an impairment of responsibility and jurisdiction. This is notably the case with the direct initiative. Anyone can draw a measure so initiated and it goes to the voters without any intermediate fact-finding, hearing, sifting, or deliberation by a public body. From the standpoint of reasoned decision-making, this is akin to the determination of a case at law by popular vote without benefit of any formal representation or consideration. The indirect initiative does afford an opportunity for legislative consideration but it usually permits of adoption of the original proposal in its pristine form by vote of the electors. It is fundamentally subject to the same objection. It is hard to see how such procedures could have other than a stultifying effect upon a representative body with general responsibility for policy-determination.

The optional referendum is negative. It does not affect directly the work of the legislature in the initiation and consideration of legislative proposals. Its psychological overhang is something that would be difficult to gauge. One would suppose that such influence as it might have would be repressive.

Perhaps there are positive values served by the initiative and referendum to which I am not sufficiently sensitive. What stands out is their part in the cumulative attack upon the legislature and representative government. I think it highly salutary that there have been no recent converts, the Model State Constitution notwithstanding.[48]

NOTES

1. See pp. 27–36 supra.
2. Mass. Const. Part the First, art. XXII.
3. American Political Science Ass'n, American State Legislatures, 89 (Zeller ed. 1954).
4. The Council of State Governments, Book of the States, 30, 38–39 (1958).
5. Id. at 38–39.
6. See Chapter I, notes 3 and 4 supra.
7. The Council of State Governments, op. cit. supra note 4, at 58, 70–71. For a discussion of the history and operation of legislative councils, see American Political Science Ass'n, op. cit. supra note 3, at 126–36.
8. Kan. Laws 1933, ch. 207, as amended [now Kan. Gen. Stat. §§ 46–301 to 315 (1949)].
9. See 12 The Council of State Governments, op. cit. supra note 4, at 36–37, for legislative pay scales.
10. Luce, Legislative Assemblies, 553 (1924).
11. The Council of State Governments, op. cit. supra note 4, at 36–37.
12. See, e.g., Pa. Const. art. II, § 8.
13. U.S. Const. art. I, § 5.
14. U.S. Const. art. I, § 7.
15. 1 Sutherland, Statutory Construction §§ 903–5 (3d ed. Horack 1943); Luce, Legislative Procedure, 211–19 (1922).
16. National Municipal League, Model State Constitution art. III, § 314 (5th ed. 1948).
17. E.g., N.Y. Const. art. 3, § 14.
18. E.g., Pa. Const. art III, § 2.
19. E.g., Ohio Const. art. II, § 8.
20. E.g., Pa. Const. art. III, § 1.
21. E.g., N.J. Const. art. 4, § 7, para. 4; Ohio Const. art. II, § 16; Pa. Const. art. III, § 3
22. Ruud, "No Law Shall Embrace More than One Subject," 42 Minn. L. Rev. 389, 447 (1958).
23. Legislative Reorganization Act of 1946 §§ 102, 121, 133, 134, 202, 203, 204, 60 Stat. 814–20, 822–30, 831–32, 834–37 (1946), as amended, 2 U.S.C. §§ 72a, 166, 223, 271, 275 (1953); Kefauver and Levin, A Twentieth-Century Congress 166–69 (1947).

24. American Political Science Ass'n, op. cit. supra note 3, at 98–100; The Council of State Governments, op. cit. supra note 4 at 30–31, 43.
25. Anderson v. Dunn, 6 Wheat. (U.S.) 204 (1821); Brown v. Brancato, 321 Pa. 54, 184 Atl. 89 (1936).
26. The Legislative Process in Congress, 299 (Thomas Y. Crowell Company, 1953).
27. 60 Stat. 835 (1946), 2 U.S.C. § 72a (d) (1953).
28. S. Rep. No. 1716, 84th Cong., 2d Sess. 2–19 (1956). See also Report on the 1957 Bricker Amendment, 12 The Record of N.Y.C.B.A. 320, 329 (1957).
29. See e.g., 2 Sutherland, op cit. supra note 15, §§ 5001–16. Pa. Stat. Ann. tit. 46, § 551 (1052), Martin Estate, 365 Pa. 280, 74 A.2d 120 (1950).
30. 2 Sutherland, op. cit. supra note 15, § 5009.
31. Bradley, Legislative Recording in the United States, 29 Am. Pol. Sci. Rev. 74 (1935).
32. Note, The Inadequacy of Legislative Recording in Iowa, 35 Iowa L. Rev. 88 (1949).
33. Note, The Use of Contemporaneous Circumstanecs and Legislative History in the Interpretation of Statutes of Missouri, 1952 Wash. U.L.Q. 265, 273.
34. Note, The Use of Extrinsic Aids in Statutory Interpretation in Kentucky, 36 Ky. L. J. 190 (1948).
35. See 7 New York State Constitutional Convention Committee, Problems Relating to Legislative Organization and Powers, 48–55 (1938), wherein it was noted that publication of the daily debates of the legislature was advocated by Elihu Root and Alfred E. Smith in the 1915 Convention.
36. New York Times (April 15, 1957), p. 28, col. 6.
37. New York Times (April 22, 1957), p. 24, col. 7.
38. Chamberlain, The Courts and Committee Reports, 1 U. Chi. L. Rev. 81 (1933).
39. 7 New York State Constitutional Convention Committee, op. cit. supra note 35, at 48–55.
40. American Political Science Ass'n, op. cit. supra note 3 at 102–3.
41. Mo. Const. art. 3, § 22.
42. For the types and duties of permanent legislative service agencies in the several states, see 12 The Council of State Governments, op. cit. supra note 4, at 61–69.
43. See, e.g., American Political Science Ass'n, op. cit. supra note 3, at 132; 7 New York State Constitutional Convention Committee, op. cit. supra note 35, at 309; Davey, The Legislative Council Movement, 1933–1953, 47 Am. Pol. Sci. Rev. 785 (1953); Asch, The Legislative Council Movement in the United States, 31 St. John's L. Rev. 49 (1956).
44. It is to be noted that paragraph 25 of U.S. House Rule XI was so

amended in 1955 as to add several of the elements of a body of rules of fair procedure for House Committees. See House Manual and Rules, H.R. Doc. No. 474, 84th Cong. 2d Sess., 364 et. seq. (1957).

45. American Political Science Ass'n, op. cit. supra note 3, at 250–53.
46. Fordham and Leach, The Initiative and Referendum in Ohio, 11 Ohio St. L. J. 495–96 (1950).
47. American Political Science Ass'n, op. cit. supra note 3, at 25–28.
48. National Municipal League, Model State Constitution, art. IV (5th ed. 1948).

III

Sanctions

of Laws and People

In a plain way of speaking, what a legislature does when it passes a law is to tell people how they are to behave. If the statute is a criminal measure, it tells everybody not to behave in a defined way—it excludes from the area of legitimate behavior whatever is defined as criminal.

Telling people what the ground rules are is one thing, getting them to comply is another. This is where sanctions are brought into play. Legal sanctions are the means employed by public authority to get people to behave as the law wants them to behave. Sanctions are, then, a function of enforcement policy. Thus, the legislature must do more than determine and articulate primary policy; it must make a choice as to means of dealing with the problems of possible and actual deviation.

In the interest of accuracy, it should be noted that some sanctions have the objective of excluding people outright from the social scene. Consider the death penalty. Apart from any revenge element, capital punishment is a means of final exclusion. Exclusion is an objective in the case of habitual offenders.[1]

It is pretty clear that the legislative institution could

be examined at great length without focusing on the area of sanctions. I am, nevertheless, emboldened to invite attention to it in this chapter. I am moved by a sense of the vital relationship of sanctions to the effectuation or fulfillment of policy. And here, reference is made not alone to the assertion of the authority of the state in one way or another to get people to comply. There is the underlying and extremely difficult process of thinking through proposed policies with due regard to the potential for conformity.

In a sense, mature consideration of the problem of achieving a high degree of compliance with policy is the test of sound lawmaking. Nothing is clearer than that no matter how noble the experiment, a desired pattern of behavior is not something simply to be willed by governmental authority; even a Hitler understood that it takes a good deal more than this. The familiar expression "there ought to be a law" may be a strong way of expressing one's personal views, but whether there should be a positive enactment is a question that involves a much more complex inquiry than even the question as to what, in the judgment of the members of the legislative body, would be morally right or socially wholesome. What it would take in the way of sanctions to influence conformity to a proposed policy bears upon the choice of that policy, as against others which might be adversely affected by its enforcement.

What I have discussed thus far is by way of preliminary. Its function is to suggest that the problem of sanctions renders all the more demanding the need of a strong state legislative institution which can give the needed consideration to the problems of the larger community, with proper regard to the social and behavioral factors which condition the attainable and bear on its desirability as a choice, in any event.

Without benefit of psychiatric thought, Jeremy Bentham and others did some rather basic thinking about the motivating influences of human conduct. Bentham identified pleasure-seeking and pain-avoiding as the chief human motivations.[2] This affords a rational basis for a system of sanctions employing rewards and punishments. Thus, in simple terms, a pain-inflicting sanction should be severe enough to overbalance clearly the "pleasure" to the individual to be anticipated by him as a consequence of deviating from the law.

Contemporary psychiatric thought embraces the proposition that the psychic processes are governed by the principle of obtaining pleasure.[3] It tells us, however, that the simple, unmodified pleasure-pain principle of human motivation does not consist with reality. Its application would result in more pain than pleasure and, thus, be destructive in its consequences. In the development of the individual personality and character, reality requires an accommodation to external standards and the interests of others.[4] This results in the shaping in the individual of conscious and unconscious restraints and responses—the development of the adult conscience, the functioning of which in itself provides more gratification. In lay terms, what the psychiatrists tell us is that the reality of the external world, and especially human values and interests, develop and temper simple, unvarnished pleasure-seeking as a motivating force.

In this perspective, what is the potential of a system of rewards in the total scheme of legal sanctions? Up to this point, nearly all legal sanctions have been and are pain-inflicting. Civil sanctions, whether in the form of damages, specific relief, or what not, are pain-inflicting in the psychic sense although not punitive as a legal matter. It must be recognized that this is a generalization, to which, from the victim's standpoint, exceptions must be noted. Some persons seek "pain" which gives psychological satisfaction. Some actually seek punishment to overcome feelings of guilt. Some want to go to an institution because it is secure and relieves them of making decisions.

As Bentham observed, something like pecuniary reward for general law observance would be out of the question.[5] A large measure of conformity there must be if a law is to be effective. We cannot pay all and sundry for being good boys. The state's moral position would be a queasy affair, moreover, if it had to hold out some specific benefit as an inducement to observe the law.

This, however, is not the whole story. Clearly, the reward principle can be used to get people to behave in a way that goes beyond that exacted by law. A familiar example is a discount for prepayment of taxes.[6] The payment of a bounty for the killing of predatory animals, like foxes and wolves, falls in this category.[7] More subtle rewards, not necessarily of a tangible character, may be employed to influence basic compliance with law. Approbation and favorable publicity may be used, as where eating establishments which have good records of compliance with sanitary and health requirements are given public notice.[8]

Ordinarily, classification becomes meaningful when undertaken for a particular purpose. Thus, the concept of public purpose may be one thing for tax exemption purposes and another for purposes of governmental entry into a particular activity.[9] A more academic approach to the classification of sanctions may be worthwhile as a means of intellectually fingering the idea currency of this subject. I resort to classification on a working basis without the slightest suggestion of final authority.

There are many possible bases of classification. I think we should begin with the public-private dichotomy. Private sanctions are those employed by private persons and groups without resort to law or governmental authority. In contrast, public or governmental sanctions involve action by governmental authority, whether judicial, legislative, executive, or administrative. The concept of public sanction is something broader than what is to be correctly identified as a legal sanction. When a legislative committee, which is conducting an investigation, tries to influence human behavior by manipulation of publicity or otherwise by its own direct action,[10] the committee is not resorting to any form of legal sanction; it is not effectuating a policy laid down by law nor is the sanction itself provided by law. Yet, it is public or governmental action.

Private, like public, sanctions are extremely varied. In defense of his person or his estate, one may use force upon another. This is charmingly expressed in the old plea by a landowner in defense of a civil action for throwing a trespasser off his land. *Molliter manus imposuit*—he placed his hand upon him gently—ran the ancient plea. Private organizations have their own systems of sanctions within their particular sovereignties. Some, like expulsion, may be drastic. Excommunication pales the term.[11]

The distinction between legal sanctions, on the one

hand, and moral, religious, and social sanctions, on the other, is not the same as public versus private. The basis of distinction here is the nature of the authority or authoritative force behind a sanction. Obviously, a particular legal sanction, as we shall observe more fully a little later, is likely to be fortified by religious, moral, or social authority.

At this point, we lay aside private sanctions, for our concern is with what public authority may do to achieve conformity to policy and especially with what may be provided for in this respect by legislation.

Sanctions may be classified as civil and criminal. If "civil" is used to indicate that a judicial proceeding in which enforcement is sought is civil in character, its usefulness is limited for there are many proceedings initiated by public authority which are civil in form but are seriously punitive in nature and effect. Such is a proceeding for the denaturalization of a naturalized citizen.[12] The classification will be important from the standpoint of the availability of procedural safeguards.[13] If "civil" is used to denote a sanction for the protection or enforcement of civil or private law relationships, the classification may have greater utility. It does not mean sanctions available only to private parties, for obviously a government may, as an owner or contracting party, for example, sustain private law relationships.

The chief conventional civil sanctions of our law, while subject to legislative modification, are judicial in origin. This is true of common-law damages and the equitable remedy of injunction. The usual recourse at common law was substitutional redress—damages. In equity, prevention and specific redress were more the order of the day. These three—damages, prevention, and specific redress—together with punishment, Roscoe Pound tells us, exhaust the possibilities of judicial action to protect interests, individual or social.[14] The three present extremely interesting differences from a policy standpoint. They afford a legislature a freedom of choice beyond conventional punitive sanctions in implementing the policy expressed in a penal or regulatory statute. Thus, injunction as a public remedy may be employed to restrain conduct punishable as a crime.[15]

When sanctions are classified as positive and negative, we have a reclassification of rewards and punishments. Here, once more, the form of proceeding is not controlling. The stress is on the nature of the effect upon the individual against whom a sanction is invoked. If the sanction is a burden or deprivation the calculated effect will be negative, whether the form of the enforcement proceeding is civil or criminal. Professor Edwin Patterson has observed that since rewards, like bounties for killing wolves, are not given for performing a legal duty, a reward is not, by prevailing usage regarded as a sanction.[16] I recognize the difference on which he relies, but it still may be said that he has not invalidated our classification. A person may be given a benefit for doing what the law requires him to do, even if nothing more than favorable publicity.

We can classify sanctions in terms of the governmental arm which exerts governmental authority. Thus, they may be legislative, judicial, or administrative, although, in the sense of ultimate physical compulsion, enforcement may be the use of physical power by a police or other official. This classification may be significant with respect to conscious consideration of the suitability of a particular governmental arm for a given enforcement responsibility.

If we look again at governmental sanctions, we see that they break down into a criminal group and a regulatory or supervisory group. We have been developing a great armory of the latter in our administrative law and practice. It is here that we encounter informal sanctions of a preliminary character, such as inspection and investigation, which may be very useful in themselves in influencing human behavior. Threat of prosecution is a significant intermediate administrative sanction.[17] It is calculated to be effective as against people of standing who value their reputations and would be concerned by the adverse impact of prosecution. That is hardly the case, as others have pointed out, with the disreputable who have no such sensibility.[18] As to them, well-conceived legal sanctions are needed to backstop the threat.

In the very broadest sense, the indispensable element of sanction in any legislation designed to order human behavior is the willingness of the members of the community at large to conform, whether by reason of approval of or acquiescence in the policy itself or by reason of a social character which impels the desired compliance with a measure which may be distasteful. One might suggest that this is just another way of saying that a legislature cannot effectively impose upon people a policy which is more than they can or will stomach.[19] We have some fairly obvious illustrations of the essentiality of this element, which are not always candidly identified. A conspicuous example is legislation to suppress gambling. There is a strong desire on the part of many worthy elements in the community to suppress gambling as an evil. Actually, what has taken place is the enactment of a good deal of legislation addressed to this practice in its various manifestations with little basis in fact for expecting a high degree of compliance. We sound the moral tone in the legislation, but the gambling goes on in one form or another. Many who recognize this are heard to say "let's legalize gambling and bring it out in the open with the dual objective of putting the crooked commercial gambler out of business and creating a source of tax revenues." I mention their thinking merely to footnote the point as to the disparity between what the law expects and what far more than a marginal few of us will do.[20]

John Dickinson has put the matter a little differently. He observed that even a badly enforced law relating to a subject like gambling does not leave the situation as it was before.[21] By deflecting a practice to a new form, the law may, he said, satisfy the dominant elements in the community somewhat better than would otherwise be the case.

While our insights into the subject of sanctions are probably less mature than those we have gained as to almost any other major aspect of lawmaking, a sanction or a pattern of sanctions is so much a characteristic part of legislation that we are wont to look upon formal sanctions as something indispensable. There is a considerable body of judicial authority to support the proposition that a municipal ordinance of a regulatory character which is not supported by a legal sanction is juridically toothless, and, as such, without legal effect.[22] This has been obviated in some instances by a rather delightful circular reasoning process. There is a familiar rule of state tort law that violation of an ordinance designed to protect people of a class may be at least evidence of negligence in a suit for personal liability or property damage by one of the class.[23] Such an ordinance without any internal sanction has been found to have vitality for purposes of this rule, since the rule itself provides the sanction to put stuff in the ordinance and thereby presents us with a valid ordinance to which the rule may refer![24]

We see this emphasis upon formal legal sanctions in the history of declaratory judgment proceedings. It took us quite a while to get it clearly established that a declaratory judgment proceeding in which the prime concern was with an adjudication of the legal relations of the parties without immediate thought of judicial sanctions was, nevertheless, an honest-to-goodness case or controversy within the judicial competence.[25] Today, of course, there is a ready appreciation of the fact that a proceeding of this character is an instrumentality of a mature legal system, which is effective in practically all cases without resort to any formal sanction. This means of making adjudications as to legal relations authoritative facilitates compliance by people disposed to be law-abiding, who otherwise might be put in a nonconformist posture.

One of the indicia of a mature legal system is its capacity to induce people to conform to legal norms without resort or even the threat of resort to the strong arm of the state. This is likely to involve a sensitive use of extra-legal sanctions as well as formal intermediate sanctions which do not involve any suggestion of employment of ultimate governmental power. Examples of the latter abound in the field of administrative law and procedure. They deserve special notice. For the moment, however, let us consider some instances of the use of extra-legal sanctions—religious, moral, and social. Not always, unfortunately, is what we do in the use of this leverage characterized by sensitivity.

A conspicuous example of the use of a religious sanction is to be found in the requirement of an oath. The amount of oath-taking engaged in in our day is staggering, if not stultifying. The very ceremonial significance of an oath tends to be lost in unrelieved commonplaceness. It is a curious commentary upon our thinking that this primitive device has such a hold upon our law and practice. I say "primitive" because there is nothing more evident to me than that the religious sanction involved in oath-taking is of this character. As I apprehend it, the oath-taker is supposed to add a grave religious sanction by invoking the wrath of the deity for deviation from the truth. What he is doing is baring his breast to Thor's thunderbolt. I should have supposed that a deliberate liar is hardly in better case in the eyes of God whether he asks for punishment or not. Of course, if our Ananias thinks that he would be in a worse position were he to be under oath, it might make a difference. The highest sanction supporting truth-telling is an inner sanction—an appreciation that truth is virtue which deserves unswerving fealty for its own sake. This is supported by the general moral sanction of the effect of infidelity to the truth upon one's character and peace of mind.

The notion that the negative quality of fear of divine or temporal punishment will motivate fidelity to truth is subject to challenge. Here, we are getting to the fundamentals of human character and one may doubt that even the avoidance of the punitive legal sanctions of perjury statutes is a reliably effective motivating force.

Of promissory oaths, such as conventional oaths of office, little could be added to what Chester Lloyd Jones has said. He declared: "The host of oaths of merely promissory character that parade through our constitutions and statute books are phantom soldiers not feared by officials and inefficient to protect the people."[26]

In the case of test oaths, such as a loyalty oath by which one disavows matters of fact which are disqualifying or derogatory, Jones contends that there is a deterrent influence. He says it stems not from fear of penalty but from a reluctance to declare in express terms that which is untrue.[27] How this differs from the situation of a witness who has just taken a promissory oath to tell the truth, he fails to make clear. Why is there more reluctance in the one case than the other?

Whether others will agree with these observations is hardly the point. I should like to see them put to the test by a thorough legislative inquiry—with the aid of competent people drawn from the social and behavorial sciences—into the significance of oath-taking as such. It would be appropriate to do this at the state level. One obvious thing to bear in mind in this connection is that, so far as the law of perjury is concerned, a false statement not made under oath can be defined as perjurous if the legislature so chooses.

The social sanction of adverse public opinion may be invoked by publicity. Being posted for nonpayment of dues is, I am told, almost as grim a prospect as the wearing of a scarlet letter. The use of it by administrative agencies is now a rather familiar occurrence. This procedure may be followed without benefit of any express statutory authorization or recognition of it. In

some areas of regulatory activity, such as protection
against impure and unsafe food and drugs, warning to
the public pending full inquiry and findings is extremely important to the effectuation of the control
policy.[28] The damaging effect of adverse publicity can
hardly be avoided. In other types of controls, which do
not relate to hazards to public health or safety, there is
a substantial policy question as to whether the legislature should permit the cognizant administrative agency
to make free use of publicity. The question arises in
acute form where the agency is using publicity to influence private conduct of one against whom it had
little or no chance of effectively invoking legal sanctions. The legislative concern here may well be more
the assurance of fair treatment to the individual than
how to get him to conform.

The social sanctions imposed against ideological deviation are one of the unhappy aspects of human relations of our time. They are our manifestation of what
has happened time and again in human history. It is to
have been expected that they would have some parallels
in legal sanctions. A ready example is the loyalty oath
exacted as a condition of public employment. Oaths
of this nature vary but they commonly involve disa-
vowal of past and present membership in a group committed to overthrow of government by force or other
unlawful means and of personal advocacy of such overthrow. This is what a group of psychiatrists have had to
say of this device, viewed from their professional standpoint:

. . . the tone of the present loyalty oaths is negative. It
places the individual's loyalty in question, it forces him to
defend it, it forces him to deny an implied accusation of

treasonable intent toward his government. In its manifest content, the current loyalty oath is threatening and coercive. In its latent content, it generates an atmosphere of accusation and suspicion.

. . . it has been amply demonstrated that the oath as a detective or deterrent agent has but little value. In fact, it is no security measure at all.[29]

If these behaviorists are close to the mark, a loyalty oath requirement is largely a product of social forces which harms law-abiding people without influencing the deviates.

Extended talk of legal sanctions, with its central focus upon conformity, makes one restive; it does not glorify the individual human spirit. The formal answer to this plaint is that the compromise or balance between conformity and individuality is struck when a policy is set by the legislature. If a rule of conduct is adopted by competent authority, thenceforth conformity is the order of the day. Viewed from the standpoint of sanctions, the problem runs deeper than this. In the first place, a thorough examination of what may be contemplated in the way of sanctions may be revealing as to the true extent and the desirability of the restriction of individual freedom of action which the measure would establish. Adequate consideration of sanctions, in short, bears on this fundamental question as well as the closely related matter of attainability or workability. Beyond this is the choice of a philosophy of encouragement and voluntariness as against a big stick philosophy in the shaping of sanctions.[30] If there must be a restrictive policy, stress on co-operation, or voluntariness, mitigates the clash between individuality and authority.

Nonconformity—freedom to dissent—is an essential

of freedom of the mind. The psychic tensions and social anxieties aggravated by the great ideological conflicts in the world today tend to impair tolerance of
thinking which deviates from the conventional. The
point has been sharply enunciated by Lawrence Z.
Freedman of the Yale Medical School:

Our society is rapidly developing a system of extra-legal
negative sanctions against those who, although they may
conform completely behaviorally, deviate in their attitudes.
Political and social crises have opened up avenues of com-
munication between groups which were formerly intellectually and ideologically isolated from each other. They
now view each other with baffled dismay. Heightened social
anxiety has obscured differences, which were formerly so
clear, between nonconformist ideas which are the private
right of man, and disloyal activities which are harmful to
the community.[31]

One of the disturbing aspects of the legislative process
on the present scene, conspicuously at the national
level, is the application of what amounts to sanctions
by legislative committees in securing compliance with
statutes or in influencing human behavior entirely in
the absence of duly established legal norms. A committee is in a position to inflict the extra-legal penalty of
exposure or adverse publicity.[32] This may result in a
further detriment, such as loss of employment.[33] There
is no question but that adverse publicity may sometimes
be unavoidable if a committee is to have relative freedom to pursue facts in a public inquiry. The disastrous
effect upon a particular individual of the exertion of
this power, which is certainly open to exploitation for
political advantage, is obvious. It presents a serious

problem, for the effect is trial by newspaper and public opinion, not by the courts under the safeguards of constitutional and lesser rules of fair procedure.

I am not disposed to suggest that the indicated corrective is limitation upon the legislative power of inquiry. Two things will help. The first is the nurturing of legislative responsibility. At the state level, this means strengthening the institution and its processes in a way calculated to develop a tradition of care, deliberation, and restraint. At both national and state levels, it means institutional resistance to use of investigatory power for ulterior ends. The second is the restraining force of public reaction against exploitation of investigatory powers.

I have already referred to administrative law and procedure as an area of governmental activity in which use may be made of means of achieving conformity without any show of authority. It is accurate to say that enforcement of regulatory laws through administration is far more a matter of education, persuasion, and exhortation than of resort to legal sanctions. Unlike criminal laws with a strong moral basis, the regulatory measure is likely to have no independent moral foundation or sanction. It is supported by the general disposition to conform to law, but there is no developed community sense of the "rightness" of the measure. The ultimate legal sanctions are needed as the "persuader of the thoroughly recalcitrant. For the rest, acceptance and compliance can be cultivated by education and genuine persuasion.

Fair employment practice laws afford an example of express statutory recognition at the state level of the potentialities of education and persuasion. What is done is to require the FEPC, once it determines that there is probable cause for a complaint that there has been an awful employment practice contrary to the act, to endeavor to eliminate the practice by conference, conciliation, and persuasion.[34] Overhanging this procedure, it is true, is the threat of formal proceedings.

The supervisory role of administrative agencies is of such great importance to the effectuation of policy that there should be special legislative interest in those agencies and the enforcement tools with which they work. The legislature is concerned with relating sanctions to policy and relating enforcement both to policy and to sanctions. Much of the content of a law is, of necessity, filled in or spelled out, as you will, in the process of application. Nowhere is this more clear than in the administration of a regulatory measure. There should be a sharp perception of this in the drafting, consideration, and adoption of a regulatory statute. There should be subsequent legislative examination of how the law is shaping up in action through review of administration. I have scant hope that there will be much done in this respect until major improvements in the standing committee system and in the legislative process generally are made.

There are areas of human activity where a very high degree of conformity is needed but we do not have strong moral or social sanctions to bolster enforcement of governmental regulation. The operation of automobiles is a ubiquitous illustration. Let's look at just one part of that area, the problem of terminal space, of parking. Dr. Jekyll leaves his office and slides behind the wheel of his car. Mr. Hyde drives off. He hurdles away down the street and, in time, arrives at his destination only to find no curb space where he may legally park. It is an awful bother to find a proper place, so he takes his chances in a no-parking zone. If he gets a ticket and can take care of it simply by paying a small fine by mail, the avoidance of inconvenience is worth it, especially in view of how things average out—you do not get caught often. Let's suppose, however, response to the ticket must be by personal appearance or that his car is impounded. This involves telling inconvenience, especially the impounding. A good sprinkling of impoundings in areas with a high incidence of illegal parking might have a very chastening effect.[35] Whether a city would choose such a ponderous operation with the not unlikely effect of cutting down the yield from a substantial source of revenue—parking fines—is another matter.

It has been said that, in studying policy choices as to sanctions, we should have a thorough knowledge of human predispositions.[36] Armed with that knowledge, we can, it is suggested, devise sanctions geared to human motivation. For some people, the problem will be one of deterrence; for others, the problem may be one of exclusion: In the latter case, the actual social need of exclusion may exist where there is no basis for it in ordinary criminal law terms—where the sanction of exclusion has a strictly preventive function. This presents serious problems as to human freedom—to institutionalize an individual as a psychopathic personality, for example, is serious business.[37] If the individual has not actually done things forbidden by law, would available knowledge of human behavior enable us to fashion and apply fairly a reliable test of potential deviation? I do not have the answer to this. If the correct answer is "no," the hazard to individual liberty would be too great to warrant resort to preventive custody. Of course, there are many otherwise "normal" persons, in their manifest behavior, who express their hostilities, frustrations, and aggressions through aggressive and illegal activity, notably in the driving of automobiles. Clearly, they should not be institutionalized, but society can act by removing or restricting their licenses to drive.

The problem of deterrence is far from simple. It cannot be met by the device of making sanctions relatively more severe. One is reminded of the story of the hanging of the pickpockets at Tyburn. The gibbeting was performed in public in order to serve as a stern warning to potential offenders. As the story runs, a great crowd assembled, the pickings were fat, and the pickpockets, who were yet at large, simply had a field day.

Doubtless, the critical factors are individual human motivation and the quality of law enforcement. For understanding of human motivation, we must depend rather heavily upon the behavioral scientist. This presents a problem for him. The psychiatrist is concerned primarily with the well-being of his patient; he is therapy-oriented. If he is to be helpful in the devising of sanctions, however, he must contribute to the making of some generalizations; we do not enact laws on an individual basis. This does not exclude some flexibility in sanctions and much greater flexibility in enforcement. The complex problem with which we are confronted is to provide a total scheme of policy, sanctions, and enforcement which will make the law in books and in action substantially even-handed but will, at the same time, be calculated to make maximum use of the deterrence potential.

Nearly thirty years ago, James M. Landis made "a plea in the name of science for a study of sanctions,"[38] a plea which he renewed in 1938.[39] On the later occasion, he expressed political as well as scientific concern with the problem. Meanwhile, the subject has been getting not a little scientific attention from political and behavioral scientists.[40] Political concern has been displayed by some lawyers, political scientists, and people engaged in public administration.[41] The subject has not, however, gained anything approaching merited consideration in legislative halls. Independent inquiry and evaluation have not been undertaken.

As Landis pointed out, we have not been lacking in ingenuity in devising sanctions. They have been developed in great variety for many different enforcement objectives. We have not, however, made a studied effort to evaluate their effectiveness and gauge their potential.

We do not find in our legislative institutions any definite machinery or methodology for giving sustained attention to the problem of sanctions. More commonly than not, some kind of conventional sanction, such as fine or imprisonment or both, will be injected into a statute in one of its closing sections without any independent consideration of its effectiveness in influencing people to conform. It may well be that this casualness will not make much difference in a particular instance as to most people affected, since they will, by social forces or personal character, be motivated to conform. It is those who are prepared to deviate for their own temporary advantage who create the problem and whose nonconformity may have a corrosive effect upon the law-abiding inclinations of others. In the process of enactment, the question whether fear of the sanctions provided would keep most potential nonconformists in line is simply not explored. There is neither a studied drawing upon the accumulated data and insights of social and behavioral scientists as well as public officials nor fresh inquiry into human behavior as related to the policy area.

Since, by resort to legal sanctions, we are undertaking to influence human behavior, would it not be wise in fashioning sanctions to make use of all that is pertinent of what is known and understood or could be determined about human motivation? If so, why not regularize the business within the legislative framework? I would answer these questions in the affirmative and would suggest that the nub of the matter is that the scheme of sanctions supporting particular legislative policy should be custom-made. If perceptive social and behavioral scientists can help with the sentencing process in the administration of justice, they, no doubt, could help here.

More specifically, I am suggesting that there be established in a state legislative body a standing committee on sanctions and law enforcement which would be competently staffed to give thoughtful and informed attention to the problem of sanctions in any substantial legislative proposal. I am prepared to assume whatever risk this proposal carries of being identified as an impractical theorist. I am perfectly willing to take that risk in an effort to draw attention to the importance of making the best use of the knowledge and trained talents that we have in a key phase of policy-making and implementation. Actually, I know of nothing more practical than such a basic approach. I do recognize that we must contend with inertia and political forces in getting such an idea across.

It will be seen that, were a committee of the indicated character and purpose established, it would have at least three important roles to play. It would have the role of testing the basic policy of a legislative proposal in terms of its attainability as a means of ordering human relations. Its second role would be the fashioning or refashioning of the scheme of sanctions devised to implement a given proposal. Its third function would be to learn as much as possible about the effectiveness of existing sanctions in the process of review of administrative performance. In all of these roles, the committee would have to work in co-ordination with regular committees which had jurisdiction over the subject-matter areas of immediate concern. In theory, each standing committee could be given the means to do these things for itself but such an elaboration of staff would be needless and insupportable. The responsibility could be rested upon a legislative reference bureau. This would not afford the advantage of directly strengthening the legislature and its operation. A standing committee within the legislative framework, which was concerned with sanctions and law enforcement, would have the status and authority to work on an equal footing with the subject-matter committees.

A committee of this nature would have a significant

potential as a check on extreme and repressive legislative proposals. It could provide some of the rational
resistance to fanaticism to which Professor Lasswell has
referred in the following statement:

Popular outbursts of hostility create an environment in
which the legislator who obtains a tactical advantage is the
one who is willing to introduce the most "absolute" bills
with the most drastic sanctioning requirements. If popular
sentiment quickly dissipates, we may hear no more of the
proposal. But some persons are prone to impose their will
on others in the name of righteousness, and push through
unenforceible statutes that give rise to chronic difficulties of
enforcement and compliance. With the speed of psychiatric
understanding such compulsive characters may not themselves be changed, but their influence may be diminished by
inducing greater resistance to fanaticism that parades in the
name of virtue.[42]

There is, indisputably, a difficult problem of com-
munication in making good use of the knowledge and
insights of social and behavioral scientists. It is not easily
overcome because their methods of thought as well as
their very terminology are different from those of
people who draft laws and people who enact them. Com-
munication is, however, likely to be improved by association and by effort in communicating. For several
years now, there have been stirrings of interest in these
matters in the law schools of the country. In a few of
them, a serious effort is being made to enrich legal education by drawing upon these related disciplines.[43] This
is but a beginning. I know from experience in the school
with which I am associated that the going is not easy.
It will not be easy in the legislative milieu, but I suggest
that there, too, it is time to make a serious start.

NOTES

1. E.g., Cal. Pen. Code §§ 667, 668 (West 1955); Mass. Gen. Laws ch. 279, § 25 (1932); N.Y. Code of Crim. Proc. § 510; N.Y. Pen. Law §§ 1940, 1941.
2. 1 Bentham, An Introduction to the Principles of Morals and Legislation, 161, 169 (1823).
3. Watson, Psychiatry for Lawyers, 29, 30 (2d mimeo. ed. 1957).
4. Ibid.
5. Bentham, The Limits of Jurisprudence Defined, 226 n.5 (Everett ed. 1945).
6. Pa. Stat. Ann. tit. 72, § 5511.10 (1950).
7. Mass. Ann. Laws, ch. 131, § 109 (1957); Ohio Rev. Code Ann. § 957.01 (1953).
8. National Institute of Municipal Law Officers, Model Ordinance Service §§ 8-1404, 1407 (1952). The Model Ordinance cited is based on those of East Chicago, Ind., Indianapolis, Ind., and Pittsburgh, Pa. See Western Pennsylvania Restaurant Association v. City of Pittsburgh, 336 Pa. 374, 77 A.2d 616 (1951), where the Pittsburgh ordinance was held valid.
9. Public Parking Authority of Pittsburgh v. Board of Property Assessment, 377 Pa. 274, 105 A.2d 165 (1954).
10. An example of this kind of conduct by congressional committees is furnished by the attempt of the late Senator Joseph R. McCarthy of Wisconsin, then chairman of the Senate Permanent Sub-committee on Investigations, to halt trade between certain countries friendly to the United States and Red China. Senator McCarthy obtained voluntary agreements from certain Greek shipowners not to deal with the Reds. He also attempted to obtain agreements from other foreign shipowners but without success. For a summary of the Senator's activities in this matter, see New York Times (April 5, 1953), § 4, p. 2, col. 1; id. (April 19, 1953), § 4, p. 2, col. 4; id. (May 10, 1953), § 4, p. 2, col. 2. See also Newman & Surrey, Legislation 244–45 (1955).
11. E.g., posting notice in a conspicuous place that a club member was delinquent in payment of his dues.
12. Immigration and Nationality Act §§ 349–57, 66 Stat. 267 (1952), as amended, 8 U.S.C. §§ 1481–89 (1953), as amended, 8 U.S.C. § 1481 (Supp. V, 1958).
13. See, e.g., United States v. Regan, 232 U.S. 37 (1914); Hepner v. United States, 213 U.S. 103, 112–15 (1909); United States v. Zucker, 161 U.S. 475, 481 (1896).
14. Pound, The Limitations of Effective Legal Action, 3 A.B.A.J. 55, 67 (1917).
15. Mugler v. Kansas, 123 U.S. 623 (1887); Heyne v. Loges, 68 Ariz. 310, 205, P.2d 586 (1949); City of Sterling v. Speroni, 336 Ill. App. 590,

84 N.E. 2d 667 (1949); State ex rel. Woodbury v. Clark, 189 Iowa 492, 178 N.W. 419 (1919); King v. Commonwealth, 194 Ky. 143, 238 S.W. 373, 22 A.L.R. 535 (1922); Ariz. Code Ann. §§ 43–4409, 4603 (1939); Iowa Code Ann. §§ 99.1, .2 (1949); Ore. Rev. Stat. §§ 465.010, .020, .110, .120 (1953).

16. Paterson, Juriprudence—Men and Ideas of the Law, 161–62 (1953).
17. Chamberlain, Dowling & Hays, The Judicial Function in Federal Administrative Agencies 85–92 (1942).
18. Id. at 91–92.
19. U.S. Const. amend. XVIII (1919); National Prohibition Act (Volstead Law) ch. 85, 41 Stat. 305 (1919); as amended, 42 Stat. 422 (1921); 45 Stat. 1446 (1929); Act of March 3, 1927, ch. 348, 44 Stat. 1381. For a frank appraisal of public attitude toward obeyance of the prohibition laws, see National Commission on Law Observance and Enforcement, Enforcement of the Prohibition Laws of the United States, H.R. Doc. No. 722, 71st Cong., 3d Sess. 48–51 (1931).
20. Deland, The Facilitation of Gambling, 269 Annals 21 (1950); Peterson, Obstacles to Enforcement of Gambling Laws, 269 Annals 9 (1950). For a proposal by former Mayor William O'Dwyer of New York City to legalize gambling in New York and the reaction of the then governor, Thomas E. Dewey, see Legalized Gambling in New York, 269 Annals 35 (1950).
21. Dickinson, Legislation and the Effectiveness of Law, 37 Rep., Pa. B.A. 337, 346–55 (1931).
22. Ex Parte Ellsworth, 165 Cal. 677, 133 Pac. 272 (1913); Coffeyville v. Vakas, 137 Kan. 797, 22 P.2d 428 (1933); Morehouse v. Hammond, 60 Utah 593, 209 Pac. 883 (1922); Pittsburgh v. W. H. Kuch Co., 21 Pa. Super. 548 (1902).
23. Caughlin v. Campbell-Sell Baking Co., 39 Colo. 178, 89 Pac. 53 (1907).
24. Hines v. Partridge, 144 Tenn. 219, 231 S.W. 16 (1921), is an example of just this kind of reasoning.
25. See Borchard, Declaratory Judgments, 132–35 (2d ed. 1941), where the history of declaratory judgments in the United States is traced, and leading cases are cited.
26. Jones, Statute Law Making in the United States 263 (1923).
27. Id. at 264.
28. Chamberlain, Dowling & Hayes, op. cit. supra note 17, at 111–13.
29. Group for the Advancement of Psychiatry, Considerations Regarding the Loyalty Oath as a Manifestation of Current Social Tension and Anxiety: A Statement Formulated by the Committee on Social Issues of the Group for the Advancement of Psychiatry and a Panel Discussion 2, 3 (G.A.P. Symposium No. 1, Oct. 1954).
30. Loss, Securities Regulation, 623 et. seq. (1951). Lee, The Enforcement Provisions of the Food, Drug, and Cosmetics Act, 6 Law & Contemp. Prob. 70, 87 (1939).

31. Freedman, Conformity and Non-Conformity, in Psychiatry and the Law 41 (Hoch & Zubin ed. 1955).
32. Watkins v. United States, 354 U.S. 178, 197–98, 199 n.32, 200 (1957), wherein the Chief Justice takes cognizance of this problem stating at 200: "We have no doubt that there is no Congressional power to expose for the sake of exposure."
33. There is the familiar situation in which a witness invokes the privilege against self-incrimination when asked about Communist associations, for example, in a public legislative hearing. Loss of employment may be a result.
34. See, e.g., Pennsylvania's Fair Employment Practice Act §§ 7–9, as amended, Pa. Stat. Ann. tit. 43, §§ 957–59 (Supp. 1958).
35. For an example of an impounding ordinance, see Philadelphia, Pa., Ordinance to Amend the Code of General Ordinances of the City of Philadelphia by Providing for the Establishment of Towing Zones; Authorizing the Removal of Unlawfully Parked or Abandoned Vehicles in Such Zones to Official Towing Stations; and Fixing Charges for the Removal and Storage of Such Vehicles in Official Towing Stations, May 31, 1956; and Philadelphia, Pa., Ordinance to Amend Section 12–2405 of the Philadelphia Code Relating to the Towing of Illegally Parked or Abandoned Vehicles, by Authorizing the Towing Away of Illegally Parked Vehicles Bearing Out-of-State Licenses Under Certain Terms and Conditions, May 5, 1958.
36. Lasswell, Legislative Policy, Conformity and Psychiatry, in Psychiatry and the Law 13, 35 (Hock & Zubin ed. 1955).
37. A Minnesota statute as to the institutionalization of sexual pschopaths was upheld in the face of due process and equal protection objections in Minnesota ex rel. Pearson v. Probate Court, 309 U.S. 270 (1940).
38. Landis, The Study of Legislation in Law Schools, 39 Harv. Grad. Mag. 433, 438 (1931).
39. Landis, The Administrative Process 121–22 (1938).
40. See the papers in Hoch and Zubin ed., Psychiatry and the Law (1955).
41. A good example is the sensitivity to problems of sanctions in the interdisciplinary effort to produce a Model Penal Code, which is being made as a project of the American Law Institute.
42. Lasswell, supra note 36, at 30.
43. Since 1955, the University of Pennsylvania Law School has been engaged in a Law and Behavioral Sciences Program with the financial assistance of the National Institute of Mental Health of the United States Public Health Service. This is an interdisciplinary effort in which the Law School is concerned with drawing upon the insights and knowledge of psychiatrists, psychologists, and others to enrich law study. It is expected that at least four volumes of educational materials for use in legal education will

come from this program. They will include a basic introduction to psychiatry for lawyers and volumes with extensive behavioral materials bearing on legal problems in the fields of criminal law, evidence, and family law. The principal participants have been two regular faculty members and a psychiatrist who is serving as a member of the faculty for the duration of the project.

The Yale Law School is now engaged in a program of this character under the same auspices. No doubt, related work is in progress elsewhere.

Conclusion

While this work has been concerned exclusively with the state legislative institution, the problem of strengthening the state legislative branch cannot realistically be isolated. It is a part of the larger problem of strengthening state government.

The extension of national responsibility and governmental activity has not been attended by a corresponding decrease in state responsibility and functions. On the whole, there has been an increase in governmental responsibilities at all levels. Nor is there basis for supposing that the total demands upon the instrumentalities of politically organized society will decrease. There is, however, very substantial likelihood that unless state government and state legislatures, in particular, are strengthened, we shall be seeing national influence and activity overrunning state inertia in critical areas of public concern. The emerging problems of our time press for attention; they will not suffer a power vacuum. If the states do not act, the national government will be called upon to find a way.

I have in mind problems of American regionalism, which embrace both the governmental problems of intrastate and multi-state metropolitanism and those of other multi-state regional configurations such as a river valley complex. These problems are on the frontier of American political life; they present the greatest and most exciting challenge to our political inventiveness and adaptability. We are talking about levels of community in which the states are in the governmental position to play leading roles. This would not, I must add, be to the exclusion of national interest and participation in any event. There is national concern with various aspects of metropolitan and regional life. The point is that the problems lie for the most part in areas of state jurisdiction and responsibility and that they are staring the states in the face.

To render them equal to the occasion, we will have to regird state governments. In most states, constitutional revision is called for. This may be a staggering political undertaking, but that warrants no compromise in the statement of the need. I am happy that it has been plainly stated by the President's Commission on Intergovernmental Relations. What is indicated, as the commission has declared, is state constitutional revision which will assume provision for "vigorous and responsible government, not forbid it."[1]

Central to the problem of state constitutional revision is the unshackling of the state legislatures and the revitalization of those bodies as trusted representative assemblies. This bespeaks restoration of those bodies to their pristine status as legislative institutions with plenary powers, the focusing of legislative responsibility in a unicameral body of modest size, and the granting of ample freedom as to the conduct of legislative business. I firmly believe in representative government. I am eager to see it work effectively in our American political system at all community levels. Right now, the legislative institution which most forcefully commands our attention is the state legislature.

We sorely need a new point of departure—a dramatic break from the unhappy situation which now obtains.

Minor tinkering with the state legislative institution would hardly be noticeable. On the other hand, major changes, such as have been suggested here, would be calculated to provide that fresh start with tonic effect.

NOTE

1. The Commission on Intergovernmental Relations, A Report to the President 56 (1955).